FLORIDA
DISASTERS

FLORIDA
DISASTERS

TRUE STORIES OF
TRAGEDY AND SURVIVAL

E. Lynne Wright

Globe
Pequot

Guilford, Connecticut

Globe
Pequot

An imprint of Rowman & Littlefield

Distributed by NATIONAL BOOK NETWORK

Copyright © 2017 by Rowman & Littlefield

British Library Cataloguing in Publication Information Available

Library of Congress Cataloging-in-Publication Data Available

ISBN 978-1-4930-2874-0 (paperback)
ISBN 978-1-4930-2875-7 (e-book)

♻™ The paper used in this publication meets the minimum requirements of American National Standard for Information Sciences—Permanence of Paper for Printed Library Materials, ANSI/NISO Z39.48-1992.

Printed in the United States of America

For George, for sharing his knowledge of things medical, maritime and Internet; for Wendy, who quietly helps in countless ways while I'm writing, then actually reads my books; for Craig, for his steadfast encouragement and extraordinary skills as a publicist; for George III, for his unending support and for supplying laughs about the writing life when I sorely needed them; and for Skipper, who loves me even when I don't have time for him.

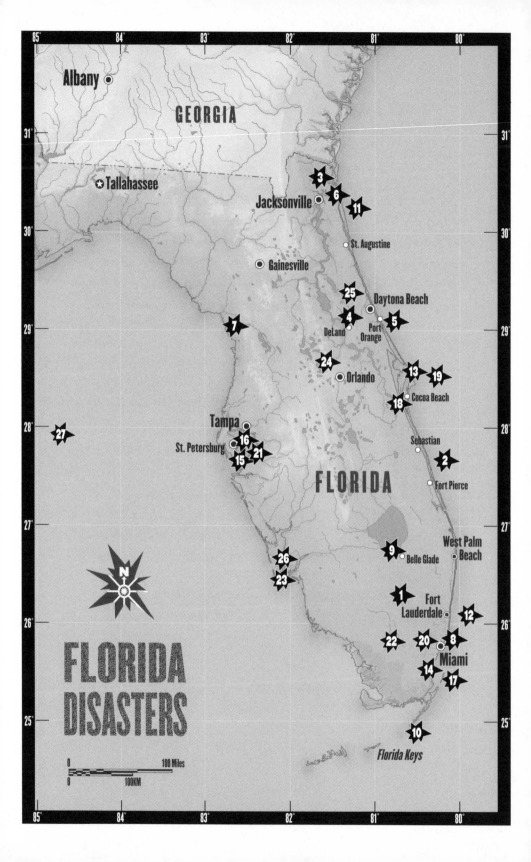

Contents

Acknowledgments

This book began with Mike Urban finding me and liking my previous . . books enough to suggest this one. I thank him for that.

Thanks to the Florida State Archives for their gold mine of excellent photographs and the assistance of their efficient staff, especially archivist Adam Watson.

I am most grateful to the librarians at the Indian River County Main Library. They are so good at their jobs, they make mine easier. Special thanks to Pam Cooper and Cyndi Davis in the Florida History and Genealogy Department.

I also thank the staff at the Cocoa Beach Public Library for their assistance in locating much information on the Harbor Cay story.

Special thanks to Tom McPherson and Peggy Kunkle at the National Museum of Naval Aviation for their expert help with the story of Flight 19.

The Jacksonville Historical Society was particularly helpful in supplying leads to track down some of the more difficult resources, and I thank them.

Ellen Henry at the Ponce de Leon Lighthouse Museum supplied me with leads on the *Commodore* chapter, and I thank her.

Thanks to Lee Fox at Save Our Seabrids for generously allowing me to use her own photos and for the outstanding work she does every day.

Thanks, too, to Catherine Lux at the American Institute of Architectural Students for her tireless efforts at tracking down those obscure files.

I am grateful to Dave Swan, Director of the Jacksonville Maritime Museum, for his fabulous detective work on the *Gulfamerica* story.

Most of all, I'm grateful to my editor, Lynn Zelem, for her kindness, intelligence, encouragement, knowledge, and talent.

Introduction

There's a saying among writers that if you want to learn about a subject, write a book about it. While researching this book, I continued my ongoing Sunshine State education and with it my ever-growing affection for this land of beaches and Seminoles, alligators and palm trees, pelicans and Mickey Mouse, NASA and the Daytona Speedway.

In addition to being blessed with 1,197 miles of coastline and 12,000 miles of rivers and streams, Florida also juts out between the Gulf of Mexico and the Atlantic Ocean like a sore thumb, so it's not surprising that our state is the scene of numerous natural disasters—hurricanes, floods, epidemics from disease-carrying insects. However, apart from these catastrophes, we do seem to have more than our share of unnatural disasters, the result of human carelessness, greed, negligence, or ignorance of the needs and hopes of people whose skin is not white.

Andrew Jackson enthusiastically accepted being at the forefront of the mistreatment of the Seminoles and other Native Americans by negotiating treaties that often forcibly removed thousands of them from their ancestral lands. In 1923 widespread belief in white supremacy resulted in the total obliteration of Rosewood, a black Florida town. The influx of thousands of Cubans during the Mariel Boatlift included criminals, drug addicts, and mental patients, but the majority were family-oriented, law-abiding citizens.

Miami's skyrocketing crime rate sparked white flight to north Florida, however, and an escalating sale of bumper stickers stating, "Will the last American to leave Miami please bring the flag."

Writing a book about disasters can be an emotional experience. As I researched each episode, I identified with the people involved, from those in long ago times to the women and men in our space program, always a source of great pride and patriotism. I grieved with the rest of the country when the *Apollo* burned and when the *Challenger* exploded, and I did so again when I wrote about them.

We don't usually find fault with acts of nature and tolerate natural disasters as sometimes being inevitable. Since it's hard to criticize an act of Mother Nature, the anger comes later. But when disasters result from human actions, bad decisions, or errors, the anger is more immediate. The Deepwater Horizon oil spill in the Gulf of Mexico took eleven men's lives, disrupted the economy of the entire region, caused the worst environmental disaster America ever encountered, and will have lasting effects for no one knows how long. And it never should have happened.

It can be hard to put ourselves into another person's shoes and understand the hardships he or she endures when we haven't experienced them ourselves. It's like seeing a picture of the Grand Canyon and thinking it's a very big hole in the ground—but then seeing the real thing takes your breath away. Disasters are like that; you can't know what it feels like until it's *your* disaster and you live through the pain or grief or loss or discomfort. Florida's horrendous hurricane season of 2004 helped Floridians understand the terror and despair our Gulf Coast neighbors feel other years.

Some of us Floridians may get a bit testy about being subjected to more than our share of disasters, but during the preparation of this book, I lost count of how many people I consulted with who shrugged, saying, "It's the price we pay for living in Paradise."

I'll second that—at least until the next hurricane.

CHAPTER 1

THEY NEVER SURRENDERED

No Peace Treaty
with the Seminoles

When Christopher Columbus arrived in the New World in 1492, there are estimated to have been hundreds of thousands of people already residing in America, some thought to have been on the continent for about ten thousand years. Believing he had come upon islands in the Indian Ocean, Columbus referred to the dark-skinned occupants of the territory as "Indians."

In what was probably the first incidence of racism in the New World, he repaid their kindness, peacefulness, and generosity by sending approximately five hundred of them on small ships to Spain. About half of them died on the way; the rest were sold into slavery. Only a few of those survived, indicating that it would be more profitable to enslave them where they were living—in America. It was the first, but far from the last, in a long line of racial disasters that would take place in the newly discovered lands.

In 1763 Britain issued a proclamation specifying that all land between the Mississippi River and the Appalachian Mountains was Indian Territory, but white land investors ignored the proclamation and wasted no time trespassing into desirable areas. Other Europeans joined the Spaniards in the New World, eagerly profiting from the use of slave labor to farm cotton, sugar, and tobacco on the fertile countryside. When, using Indian slaves, Georgia mines began to generate impressive amounts of gold every day, the rush for Southern lands escalated.

The Seminoles were not the earliest Indian inhabitants of Florida and were not a distinct tribe. They were made up mostly of Creeks and other scattered Alabama and Georgia tribes, some of those having been decimated by diseases spread from the Europeans and from the effects of warfare. Included in the vast Seminole mixture were large numbers of black-skinned people—escaped slaves and their descendants who were totally accepted among the Seminoles and came to be considered members of the "tribe."

For more than fifty years, Seminoles hunted, traded, farmed, and did well in northern Florida. They then endured the next fifty years of treaties signed with and broken by whites, being cruelly driven from their northern homelands down to the center of Florida, and finally forced to the southern end of the peninsula.

From 1607, when Jamestown was settled in present-day Virginia, until the 1890s, the Indian wars were the scenes of some two hundred battles and more than three hundred treaties signed under pressure from whites and then broken by them. Indians were repeatedly coerced into signing agreements, but when they were inadequately paid the promised sums for their lands, they refused to leave, resulting in countless fierce battles. Whites who fought the Revolutionary War against England for liberty and equality chose to deny it to the natives whose skin was darker than theirs.

While the country was already involved in the War of 1812, sometimes called the Second War of American Independence, against Great Britain, U.S. troops advanced into Seminole territory in Florida, determined to penalize the natives for harboring escaped slaves and also to support the never-ending desire of whites for more land. Increased incidents and frequent military excursions into hostile regions turned into the First Seminole War in 1818, notable for General Andrew Jackson assembling some 3,500 troops who killed nearly 900 fighters, made prisoners of hundreds of women and children, and burned the natives' towns, destroyed their crops, and seized or drove off their livestock.

Florida had been a Spanish possession for nearly three hundred years, but within a few months, Jackson destroyed Seminole villages and Spanish forts. Before a year had passed, Spain had signed over Florida along with all the rest of their territory as far west as the Rocky Mountains, charging the United States the bargain rate of five million dollars. In another year, those Jackson had vanquished must have been dismayed to learn he had been named the first provisional governor of Florida. They surely would have agreed with those who a few years earlier had named their mutual conqueror "Sharp Knife" and were probably relieved to hear that he held that office for just three months before returning to his home in Tennessee, where he collapsed from severe fatigue, spitting blood from a bad cough and experiencing a dangerous weight loss. He managed to recover, however, and went on to serve in the U.S. Senate and then as president.

Jackson had a mistrust and hatred of Indians for most of his life, and so it was not surprising that long before he became president in 1829, he was a strong advocate of removing Indians to the lands west of the Mississippi. He was influential in brokering nine treaties in ten years to obtain lands forcibly vacated by Indians. In his first year as president, he moved quickly. After intense debate in Congress, on May 28, 1830, he signed the Indian Removal Act, which removed Indian tribes from Southern states where they were settled in exchange for unsettled territory west of the Mississippi.

Most prominent among the treaties signed with the Seminoles after the Indian Removal Act became law were the Treaty of Moultrie, under which the Seminoles gave up twenty-eight million acres of land for the sum of fifteen thousand dollars and some minor annuities; the Treaty of Payne's Landing, which obligated the Seminoles to abandon their four million acres within three years for a sum that amounted to two cents per acre; and the Treaty of Fort Gibson, when six Seminole inspectors were sent to Oklahoma to check areas where their reservations would be located and almost certainly did not understand the magnitude of the treaty terms or that other tribes would share their new lands.

There were numerous pacts, all of which would move the Seminoles off their territory and none of which would result in good endings for them. When the Treaty of Fort Gibson was signed by seven Seminole chiefs in 1833, the government claimed the Seminole delegation that inspected the lands consigned to their nation had subsequently agreed that their people would migrate to Indian Territory. That assertion was denied by the chiefs, who claimed they were only to have inspected the territory, report back to their people, and consult with them before announcing a decision as to whether the Seminole people would accept the move. There was disagreement among the Seminole people too. Some who felt resistance was hopeless reluctantly agreed to emigrate, while others, including a young warrior named Osceola, passionately opposed the relocation.

Osceola was especially infuriated to learn the treaty dictated that the escaped slaves who had lived among and intermarried with Seminoles were to be re-enslaved. According to one enduring legend, when the chiefs who were to sign the Treaty of Fort Gibson gathered around the treaty lying on a table, Osceola stabbed it with his knife, snarling, "This is the only treaty I will ever make with the whites."

Fiercely hostile to the agreement, Osceola accosted one of the Indian delegates, who was on his way home from signing the treaty. Osceola killed him and recovered the pouch of gold on his body— payment for the Seminoles' leaving the land. Saying that no Seminole blood must ever be bought, Osceola scattered the gold coins on the ground and left the body to rot or be devoured by wild animals. Word spread, and within three weeks, aroused Seminoles attacked a military baggage train. On December 28, 1835, the Second Seminole War had begun.

Lasting from 1835 to 1842, it was the longest and most disastrous of the so-called Indian Wars. The Indians battled not only for their lands and for justice but also for the rights of the blacks who lived among them and the descendants of those blacks, who considered themselves to be Seminoles even though they were not aboriginal. The United States lost at least 1,500 regular soldiers and unknown numbers of volunteers, plus an estimated forty million dollars in property and other damages. Nearly four thousand Seminoles who survived the war moved west to Oklahoma, but three hundred exhausted and undefeated natives defiantly retreated deep into the Florida Everglades.

The leader of this remaining band was Holata Micco (or "Billy Bowlegs," as he was known to the whites). When surveyors were sent into the Big Cypress Swamp, they discovered the Seminoles had an impressive garden of fruits and vegetables. They harvested huge amounts of the crops and destroyed the rest, offering no payment or apology. It was the last straw for Bowlegs and his people. They attacked the surveyors in the morning, beginning the Third Seminole War.

This Seminole War was different in that it never really ended. The Indians who made the swamp their home used guerilla tactics and were able to survive in the marshland, as no whites managed to do. In 1858 the Seminoles were offered payments, which were accepted by some and flatly rejected by about three hundred, who scattered to the Big Cypress Swamp, the Everglades, and the Ten Thousand Islands.

Those who did relocate to the West had to endure the hardship of starting their lives over in unfamiliar and unsettled surroundings amid attacks from other tribes competing for scarce resources to survive, while all struggled to become accustomed to the ways of their conquerors.

Those who never surrendered were forced from their homes into some of Florida's most undesirable terrain—among alligators, snakes, mosquitoes, and accompanying diseases. But some made it. They did not sign a peace treaty. They never surrendered. They were not vanquished. Through some three hundred years, countless battles and mostly broken treaties, money and lives lost, the first major racial disaster in U.S. history took its shameful place.

CHAPTER 2

DISASTER ON THE TREASURE COAST

The Wrecks of the Plate Fleet
1715

Much of the blame for one of the worst maritime disasters of all time must be placed at the royal feet of a mentally unbalanced king and the willful, demanding woman he chose as his second wife. King Philip of Spain had long been known as lazy and moody, but the death of his first wife caused him to become so melancholy that a search was instituted all over Europe to find a new wife for him. Within seven months he was married again. His new wife, Elizabeth Farnese of Parma, was well educated but bossy and controlling, and she refused to consummate the marriage until she received an enormous dowry that included an abundance of precious jewels.

For a long time Spain had been the most powerful nation in Europe, but as the result of years of costly war, and also the fact that she manufactured nothing other countries wanted, her economy was nearly in ruins. Because of this Spain had riches shipped to her from the New World once or twice each year. Making the journey in the summer of 1715, the ships of the Plate Fleet were also under orders to carry an opulent dowry to the impatient King Philip.

The Plate Fleet, so named because an important part of its cargo was rare Chinese porcelain tableware, actually consisted of two separate fleets. One, the *Galeones,* commanded by Captain General Don Antonio de Escheverz y Zubiza, would sail to Cartagena, Colombia, for a shipment of goods from Colombia and Peru. The other, the *Flota,* under the command of General Don Juan Esteban de Ubilla, sailed for Vera Cruz to load up material from Mexico and pick up trade goods that had been shipped there from Manila. The fleets were scheduled to meet in Havana and sail together to Spain. Due to limited space for freight, a French ship, the *Grifon,* was commissioned by the governor of Havana to join the fleet and carry cargo for him. Because of the lingering hostility between Spain and France, the *Grifon*'s captain, Antoine Darie, was not welcomed by the Spaniards, and the ensuing wrangling between them caused extra delay.

It was one more holdup in a series of them, the last being the loading of eight chests of precious valuables for King Philip into Ubilla's private stateroom, further increasing the pressure from Spain to rush home. Commander Ubilla also was well aware that hurricane season in the region had already begun, so he must have been annoyed when, at the last minute, a wealthy nobleman caused one more delay. The nobleman was huge, had a severe case of gout, and was confined to a sedan chair. One hundred barrels of water had to be removed from the ship to accommodate him and his baggage, not a good trade. Commander Ubilla was understandably irritated and anxious to embark.

Finally, on July 24, 1715, eleven Spanish ships, plus the single French ship, led by the flagship, *Capitana,* hauled in their great iron anchors and set sail. After leaving Havana they planned to navigate through the Florida Straits and follow along the east coast of Florida until the trade winds and the Gulf Stream carried them home to Spain.

Along with the *Capitana,* commanded by General Ubilla, the Plate Fleet was made up of the *Santo Cristo de San Roman,* the *Nuestra Señora de la Concepción,* the *San Miguel, El Ciervo, La Holandesa, El Refuerzo,* the *Urca de Lima,* the *Nieves,* the *Maria Galante,* and bringing up the rear, Escheverz's galleon, the *Nuestra Señora de Carmen y San Antonio.* With the commander leading the way and Escheverz, who would command in case of a battle, at the rear, it was felt the fleet was more secure. Ships known to be carrying treasure always had to be on guard against pirates.

Armed with eighty cannons, the flagship's cargo consisted of nothing but treasure. The other ships carried some gold and silver, emeralds and amber, tanned hides, vanilla and cocoa beans, copper, spices, Chinese porcelain, and tobacco.

Along with their crews, the ships carried an assortment of passengers, among them were merchants, families, missionaries, and government officials. Settling in for the long voyage, some of the men fished and the women sewed and cared for the children, who had a fine time playing among the ropes and chains and pulleys. People tended to want to stay on deck as much as possible since the old wooden ships all leaked even in good weather and were uncomfortable below. The disagreeable smell from penned livestock was not the worst of it. No matter what the weather, water seeped between cracks and seams, and after a while clothing, bedding, everything was damp and never dried out. As the voyage continued, food went bad, clothes were unwashed, as were the people, drowned rats decayed in the filthy bilge, and even with fumigation between trips, the foul smell never completely went away.

The hardworking crews were always busy, controlling the sails, tending the passengers as well as the officers, standing watches, and caring for the livestock.

Passengers enjoyed the first few days of calm, but on Sunday, July 28, the sky darkened with menacing clouds and great swells roiled the sea. The captains ordered their crews below to better secure the cargo. Crew members who were veterans of other voyages muttered among themselves, knowing a storm was coming, certain it would be a bad one. By noon it was so dark Ubilla ordered all ships to stay close and to fasten lighted lanterns high so that the ships would be visible to one another. A vial of snake oil that Captain Echeverz kept in his stateroom as his own private weather forecaster turned cloudy—not a good sign.

The waves grew higher as the winds grew stronger, screaming through the masts with a terrible shrill sound. Although Captain Ubilla usually ordered reduced sails to slow the speed of the ships for safety at night, the fleet was in a hazardous position in the Florida Straits, and in an attempt to move through quickly, he ordered full sails. By nightfall the winds gusted to 100 knots. Ships in the scattered fleet could not see one another, nor could they hear anything but the sound of the breakers smashing on the reefs, a terrifying sound even to the most seasoned sailors. The crews, resigned now to being ship-wrecked, frantically tried to loosen the lifeboats, not an easy task with the ships being tossed about so violently.

The storm had turned into a hurricane, with winds of more than 120 miles per hour. Captain Ubilla ordered all vessels to head into the wind, trying to avoid the treacherous reefs, but the mountainous 50-foot waves crushed and pushed the ships like toys ever closer to the shoals.

As the wind blasted through, sails ripped completely from their masts, the masts crashed and splintered, the screams of the men crushed underneath them went unheard in the maelstrom. Terrified livestock jammed onto the deck among equally terrified people. Priests tried to lead people in prayer, but no one could hear and most were beseeching the Almighty in their own way.

General Ubilla's flagship was first to go. With her rudder and mast gone, she was unable to make any attempt to save herself. As she smashed against the shoals, she tore apart, spilling her crew and cargo into the jagged reef of rocks. In an instant Ubilla and his crew of 223 were gone, and Echeverz with his crew of 124 followed soon after, and then the ships went, one by one, until 700 people were missing. Even when some did survive and manage to crawl up on the beach, most were sucked back again into the violent sea.

Eleven ships were lost during the nightmare, along with nearly half their crew members. Only one ship of the Plate Fleet survived the catastrophe; the French captain had taken his ship more to the northeast and entirely missed the storm. As dawn broke survivors beheld a scene littered with bodies and wreckage as far as their eyes could see. Actually, it was scattered across 30 miles of barren, unpopulated beach. It would be some time before survivors became aware that the other ships had met with the same fate as theirs and no help would be coming from them.

The highest ranking remaining officer, Admiral Don Francisco Salmon, ordered some men to search the beach and to gather up whatever might be useful to the survivors. When three lifeboats were found, he assigned other men to repair them, then sent one boat more than 100 miles to St. Augustine, the other to Havana, to seek help.

When the lifeboats were under way, Admiral Salmon set up two camps, a difficult job with almost no tools available, but using the few they found among the wreckage, exhausted work parties somehow slashed out a clearing on the dunes, built lean-tos with palm fronds, and kept fires burning at all times despite the heat. In addition to acting as a signal to passing ships, fire was also necessary to help keep swarms of insects from devouring them.

Hurricanes usually clear the air after they pass through an area, and the one they had experienced did just that. One of the repaired lifeboats was able to reach St. Augustine in three days, the other landed in Havana in only ten days. As soon as the boats reached their destinations, help was dispatched, but not quickly enough for some survivors. Some died from disease, others from exhaustion.

Salvage efforts were begun immediately, but those too proved to be a challenge, as the wreckage was spread over such a great area.

When a Spanish salvage expert, Sergeant Major Don Solorzanol, arrived, he quickly introduced an operation that proved to be dangerous and unpopular with the mostly Native-American divers. Although his methods were effective, they cost lives. Battling sharks and barracuda was not the only difficult part of the job. To hold their breath for three minutes while digging chests and other parcels out from under 6 inches of sand that had been washed over them by the storm was not for any but the sturdiest men. Then there was the matter of hauling treasure, sometimes in heavy chests, back up to the surface. There were many "unfortunate incidents," and mortality rates climbed.

Even in those times, word spread rapidly, and before long the scene of the maritime disaster was also a scene of friction. Pirates and treasure seekers came from everywhere, stealing from one another and using every kind of subterfuge to outdo their competitors. Men brought silver in large quantities up from the bottom of the sea, but the work was hard and the attacks by wildlife and by pirates were discouraging. After three years Spain gave up, torched the exposed portions of the remaining vessels, and abandoned the underwater portions to sea life and waves.

The remains of some of the Plate Fleet are still unaccounted for, which is not unusual in Florida's coastal and river waters. In fact there are believed to be over 2,000 unrecovered shipwrecks around the state, ranging from ancient galleons to boats used by modern drug runners. Interest in the Plate Fleet was revived in the 1960s by Kip Wagner, a Florida house builder, who was casually interested in lost treasure. He read up on it, bought a surplus metal detector, and when he found a gold ring, he was hooked. Becoming convinced in time that he was on to something special, he founded a salvage company that recovered countless treasures from the bottom of the sea near the area where the Plate Fleet survivors had camped.

Reports of his success stirred up renewed interest in the lost riches, and were largely responsible for naming the area bound on the north by Sebastian and on the south by Fort Pierce, the Treasure Coast. Much treasure still lies beneath the water as evidenced by the coins or other artifacts that turn up on the beaches after severe storms. However, the wrecks of the Plate Fleet are protected by admiralty claims, which means a metal detector cannot be used in the water, although it is permissible on the shore. In addition, if any treasure is found on land, it belongs to the finder. However, the state is entitled to 25 percent of any treasure found in the water on the state's submerged land.

In 1715 Elizabeth Farnese was apparently satisfied with the dowry Philip was able to provide for her. She married him, and lost no time in exerting her influence over him to the point that it was really she who controlled the country. She gave him heirs, and during Philip's later years, when it was said he was "nearly an imbecile," she ran things in such a way that she ensured thrones for both her sons and her two stepsons from Philip's first marriage.

CHAPTER 3

DISEASE SPREADS LIKE FIRE

The Yellow Fever Epidemic
1888

The heartbreaking truth is that the yellow fever epidemic that took thousands of lives and paralyzed the city of Jacksonville in the summer of 1888 need never have happened. In an age when disease was attributed to uncleanliness, noxious effluvia, or Divine Providence, the medical profession did not consider the theory of Dr. John P. Wall credible. As early as 1873, Dr. Wall had conducted experiments that led him to conclude the *Aedes aegypti* mosquito carried the disease that killed his wife and daughter two years previously in a Tampa yellow fever epidemic. When a Cuban physician, Dr. Carlos Juan Findlay, confirmed Dr. Wall's conclusions in 1881, he too was ignored.

So the stage was set when, near the end of July, R. D. McCormick, a visitor who arrived by train from Tampa, registered at Jacksonville's Mayflower Hotel. Shortly after checking in, Mr. McCormick suddenly felt terribly ill, and after being examined by local doctors, he was diagnosed as having yellow fever.

Within a few days four more cases were diagnosed, and then it seemed new cases popped up nearly every hour. Initially, the Jacksonville Board of Health tried its best to maintain calm by

Fires burning on Bay Street, deliberately set to destroy whatever carried the fever.
FLORIDA PHOTOGRAPHIC COLLECTION/FLORIDA STATE ARCHIVES

quashing any news about the disease, but by August 10 it had no choice. The board made the grim announcement that Jacksonville was experiencing a yellow fever epidemic.

Concerned citizens immediately formed the Jacksonville Auxiliary Sanitary Association to aid their civic leaders. Although it had no legal authority and worked as an auxiliary branch of the Jacksonville Board of Health, the association was extremely effective; its members worked tirelessly, carrying most of the responsibilities throughout the ordeal.

In order to forewarn people, yellow flags with the words YELLOW FEVER were placed on houses where infected people lived. However, as the disease spread, that was given up—there were just too many cases. One doctor was of the opinion that two of the thirty cases of so-called "society fever" that had been reported in February had actually been yellow fever. A few other suspicious cases were said to have been treated as well.

Many people hurriedly left the city, but the Board of Health announcement further increased anxiety to such an extent that all outgoing ships and trains were packed to capacity, some people clinging to the roofs of train cars in their desperation to escape. Refugees in wagons and on foot clogged the roads, but they soon encountered town after town refusing them entry, Jacksonville citizens having been rigidly quarantined by armed patrols as far north as St. Augustine. Neighboring Waycross, Georgia, even threatened to tear up their railroad tracks if any refugees tried to pass through their town inside locked cars. The Clyde Steamship Company stopped service to the city. Sheriff Napoleon Bonaparte Broward telegraphed his wife, who was visiting in New York City, telling her to remain there for safety.

Further, St. Augustine refused mail posted in Jacksonville, whether it was fumigated or not. Jacksonville refugees who had escaped before the quarantine was put into effect told of receiving mail from family members with holes punched into the envelopes for the sulphur fumes to penetrate.

Isolated from the outside world, Jacksonville became a grim place for the unfortunate ones who remained. Just as Jacksonville mail was refused in some places, so too was merchandise, machinery, ice, and hard currency. Banks closed as business, education, and commerce abruptly stopped. To combat soaring unemployment, the Jacksonville Auxiliary Sanitary Association organized a Public Improvement Works plan to put men back to work and to complete some badly needed municipal projects. One job they took on was to widen and improve the Evergreen Cemetery road, which had been in poor condition and was rapidly growing worse from constant use.

Along with widespread unemployment, food shortages made their appearance. The quarantine was in place for some time before it was decided to allow farmers to deliver their produce into the city during daylight hours only. People avoided being outside after dark because it was believed the best way to evade whatever carried the fever. When people did venture out during daylight hours, many wore kerchiefs over their faces, hoping to keep out whatever it was that caused the disease.

Since hotels and restaurants were closed, adding to the difficulty people had in getting meals, citizens formed eating clubs to promote sharing basic staples.

The Mayflower Hotel, which had been guarded, was condemned and burned to the ground under the authority of the fire department. Several buildings that had housed fever patients also were burned to the ground by arsonists, and even hospitals received threats of arson.

The huge warehouse of the temporarily nonfunctioning Clyde Steamship Company became a storehouse for relief supplies, including special foods and necessities, such as cots, linens, and mattresses to replace bedding that was being burned because there was no effective way to disinfect it. A carload of apples from Winsted, Connecticut, arrived at the warehouse, to be repackaged and distributed to patients in the belief that a baked apple was one of the few things that could be enjoyed by a convalescing fever patient.

Sheriff Broward, who worked tirelessly trying to keep order with a workforce depleted by the fever, received a warning that a group of dissatisfied workers were planning to break into stores. He effectively reinforced security.

Eventually, the city reached the point where authorities and citizens would try almost anything to rid the city of the calamity that had befallen it. Some unemployed men were hired to clean out ditches and fumigate the streets. Pine wood and tar blazed in barrels to purify the night air. When someone brought it to the attention of authorities that some streets were paved with cypress blocks similar to paving bricks, and that cypress swamps were considered unhealthful, the cypress blocks were immediately disinfected.

Streetcars were fumigated on a daily basis. City watering carts sprayed the streets with a solution of bichloride of mercury. The

Board of Health voted to provide $500 for the cleaning and flushing of all city sewers.

In 1877 prior to the epidemic, a prominent woman writer claimed that the explosion of gunpowder in a room would kill mosquitoes and microbes by concussion. Beleaguered Jacksonville officials imported four cannons from Castillo de San Marcos fort at St. Augustine. They fired 200 blanks at intervals downtown after dark, damaging some storefront glass and some church windows but having no effect on the deadly microbes.

Among the other efforts made to stamp out the disease was having men spray houses where yellow fever patients were with copper, sulphur, and lime, but the only discernible result of that was the overpowering smell it caused. One man said he heard that champagne was a preventative and accordingly purchased a half dozen bottles and told friends about it. One friend expressed an interest in trying out the "vaccination," so the two men set about testing the medical theory. Apparently neither contracted the disease but both admitted to severe headaches the next day.

As deaths continued to mount, coffins became scarce, necessitating some common burials outside the city. There seemed to be no end to the agony.

With all their doctors and nurses so badly overworked, Dr. Neal Mitchell, the president of the Board of Health, sent a desperate call for help to other parts of the country. Brave volunteers, nurses and doctors, arrived. In all 837 nurses and 16 physicians heeded the call, but some promptly became infected. In all 5 physicians and 8 nurses died.

On September 27, the Board of Health published its prescribed method for the treatment of yellow fever. It was as follows:

Give a hot mustard foot bath with the patient in a chair under a
blanket for fifteen minutes. After drying under the blanket place
the patient in bed with hot water bottles. Give five grains of

calomel to adults and one-half this amount to a child. After three
or four hours give a dose of castor oil or salts, also warm drinks of
orange leaf tea. After the medicine acts, give one-half teaspoonful
of nitre in cool water every two hours and an enema if necessary.
Give three tablespoonsful of beef or chicken broth or gruel and
discourage vomiting.

By early September just 14,000 of the 25,000 full-time residents
remained in the city, but by then most were destitute; all were depen-
dent on the handouts provided by the Jacksonville Auxiliary Sanitary
Association. Overseen by a former Jacksonville mayor, Patrick
McQuaid, the association dispensed bacon, flour, molasses, grits, coffee, soap, and other necessities to the needy, 196,538 life-saving rations
in all. McQuaid was quoted as saying:

> I lost one of my clerks who slept in my house. The situation is now
> terrible—over 150 new cases yesterday and 20 deaths. I hope it is
> now at its worst. At this rate the material will soon be exhausted.
> We took a census two weeks ago and found 10,000 colored and
> 4,000 whites in the city. We have to feed from six to eight thou-
> sand people daily, but the money comes in liberally, and I don't
> think we will lack for that—although at least 2 months yet have to
> be provided for, all business and work is suspended and the work
> population can't earn a cent, but for our auxiliary association I
> don't know what would have become of the people. The Board of
> Health is helpless and the city government is virtually defunct, the
> heads having fled. . . . God knows where the end is.

In special cases doctors were permitted to prescribe certain deli-
cacies for patients, but as is often the case, there were people who
found a way to take advantage of the situation. When a doctor would
accidentally leave an empty space above his signature, a patient could

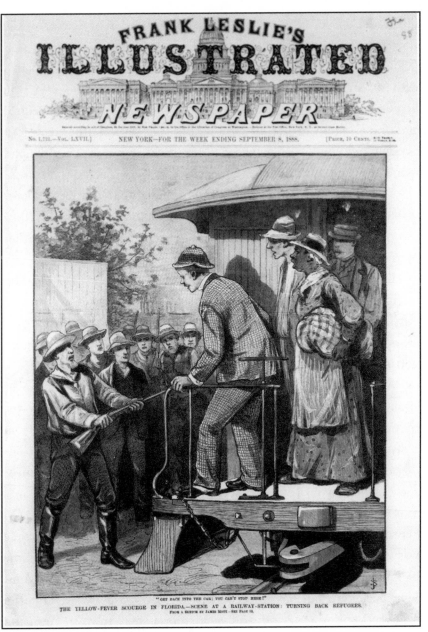

FRANK LESLIE'S ILLUSTRATED NEWSPAPER

No. 1,721.—Vol. LXVII.]   NEW YORK—FOR THE WEEK ENDING SEPTEMBER 8, 1888.   [PRICE, 10 CENTS.

"GET BACK INTO THE CAR; YOU CAN'T STOP HERE!"

THE YELLOW-FEVER SCOURGE IN FLORIDA.—SCENE AT A RAILWAY-STATION: TURNING BACK REFUGEES.
FROM A SKETCH BY JAMES MOTT.—SEE PAGE 53.

Refugees trying to escape yellow fever are turned away at a railroad station.

fill in the space. One patient inserted "6 bottles of claret," while another prescribed "12 chickens" for himself.

The *Times-Union* newspaper struggled to publish one daily paper, with its staff reduced from twenty-five to six, on good days. On September 2 the paper suspended all operations. Only the editor and one assistant had reported for work. On several other days four overworked employees managed to produce a newspaper. One staff member eventually lost to the disease was Edwin Martin, the editor.

The Savannah *Morning News* reported a prominent local doctor stated that from his vast experience in caring for patients with yellow fever, he believed redheads were immune to the disease. Several other physicians agreed with him.

But gradually, the idea gained credence that the only solution might be to move everyone out of the city. Three camps were set up outside the city, but the accommodations were meager, with used tents that were no longer waterproof, lack of blankets or mosquito netting, bad food, and no medical care.

Although people in other parts of the country were adamant about keeping the citizens of Jacksonville away from their doors, they were exceedingly generous in offering their assistance—from a distance—in the form of money and supplies. At first the citizens of Jacksonville politely declined any help, believing they could manage on their own. But as the crisis continued to become more and more overwhelming, it became necessary to seek outside help. On September 5, a call went out. In typical American fashion Jacksonville was overwhelmed again—this time by the generosity of the same people who had kept them away from their borders with shotguns. Financial contributions poured in from forty-two states; Ontario, Canada; London, England; and even from a small town in Germany. The largest contribution was from an anonymous New Yorker, later identified as being Levi Morton, who was at the time a candidate for vice president of the United States.

An unusual benefit was held in the Opera House in Atlanta for the benefit of Jacksonville. It was a spelling bee that drew a full house and netted yellow fever sufferers $700.

As was hoped, the epidemic began declining in October with gradually cooling air. When temperatures dropped to freezing four days after Thanksgiving, the ordeal seemed to be finally ending. To keep refugees from returning too soon, guards cordoned off the city, allowing only farmers and others with permits to return. No one was allowed into their home until it was fumigated, a job completed by 150 men with sixty city wagons.

By December 15 extra boats, trains, and wagons began returning people to the city, their homecoming joy diminished by memories of lost relatives and friends. In all 4,704 people had contracted the disease; 427 died. Of that number 67 were members of the Jacksonville Auxiliary Sanitary Association, which was disbanded in April 1889 after receiving commendations from Congress and the president of the United States.

CHAPTER 4

A GROWER'S NIGHTMARE

The Great Citrus Freeze
1895

Henry A. DeLand had become a wealthy man, supremely satisfied with his life, founding and running a successful baking soda manufacturing business in Fairport, New York. It was during a winter vacation when he visited his sister who lived near Daytona, Florida, that he became so impressed with that area—the beauty, the climate, the possibilities for growth and economic prosperity—that he decided to sell his business in New York, move south, and start a brand new town, to be named after himself.

He bought large parcels of land to resell to growers and others interested in investing in the area. Determined to be a responsible founder, he built a church, a post office, and several houses, and donated a swathe of land for the town's main street. He planted the streets with live oaks, knowing that in time they would form dense canopies to provide shade. DeLand enticed grocery and clothing merchants, other shopkeepers, and bankers to locate in his town, then established a school that he named DeLand Academy. He succeeded in attracting residents to the area from all over the East Coast, including his friend, John B. Stetson, the well-known Philadelphia hat manufacturer. As Stetson became more and more involved with the academy and contributed a great deal of time and money to it, DeLand honored his friend by changing the name to Stetson Academy. In time it grew into Stetson University.

Not only did the confident Mr. DeLand guarantee buyers of his land a yearly citrus harvest, he generously included in his deals a promise to buy plots back from anyone who was unhappy with their investments. It was this cool self-assurance and generosity that would lead to the loss of his fortune.

Christmas Day in 1894 was the kind of day Floridians, even in those days, liked to brag about—sunny and clear, with the temperature in the eighties. Many Central Floridians happily went swimming on Christmas morning. There was no hint of the devastation that was on the way, but within twenty-four hours, the thermometer dropped sixty degrees, the cold arriving so fast that forecasters did not have time to issue warnings. Stunned Floridians were no longer bragging. Tampa recorded 18 degrees, Jacksonville registered 14 degrees and in Palm Beach, with a temperature of 30 degrees, ice ⅛ of an inch thick was discovered in the fountain at Henry Flagler's posh Royal Poinciana Hotel. The U.S. Weather Bureau announced the unthinkable—a frost in Key West.

Water pipes froze, then burst. One woman reported waking up and hearing eggshells cracking as the eggs froze on her kitchen table. Another said her neighbor woke up, saw his ruined groves, and took a chill and returned to his bed, seriously ill.

The freeze lasted thirty-six hours, just long enough to wipe out the entire citrus crop in Central Florida. A temperature of twenty-six degrees for three or more hours freezes the juice in oranges, rendering them inedible. In the groves oranges froze on the branches, dropped to the ground, and rotted. The headline on December 29 in Jacksonville's *Daily Florida Citizen* read, "Ice and Snow in Florida." On December 30, it said, "It Is a Story of Ruin."

Citrus crop destroyed after the freeze.
FLORIDA PHOTOGRAPHIC COLLECTION/FLORIDA STATE ARCHIVES

Florida had been regarded as being close to a genuine Utopia by families who lived year-round in the central part of the state, most of whom were in some way involved in citrus growing. Many of these hardest hit small growers had no choice but to leave the Sunshine State and return north in order to survive. Tourists also departed, but most large growers were determined to hang on, looking forward to the following year.

The freeze was a crushing blow but not a complete catastrophe. Although the fruit on the trees was ruined, the trees survived and quickly began to recover as the air warmed. With January's mild weather, the trees' new growth continued developing normally, and it seemed to be nearly back to where it should have been by the end of the month. Growers allowed themselves to be lulled into the comfortable feeling that they had survived the worst and it was nearly over.

Word spread that southern Florida was not at all affected, as attested to by a farmer who wrote to the Titusville newspaper, reporting the Biscayne Bay area "is not frozen out as yet, as will be shown by the shipments of tomatoes made this month. Between 200 and 300 crates will be shipped from here tomorrow. . . . The cold did little damage here. . . . The leaves on the banana trees are burnt some, but the fruit is not injured. . . . we will have a full crop of tomatoes."

Similar remarks from others in southern Florida stirred some growers' interest toward that part of the state, but when January brought warmer weather, hope was renewed in Central Florida. Few people realized that as the citrus trees began to recover—trunks filling with sap, buds forming, even some white blossoms appearing here and there—the trees were at their most vulnerable.

Then on February 7 hopes were demolished along with the trees as an even worse freeze hit the area, plunging the temperature into the teens. For two days the temperature stayed below freezing in two-thirds of the state.

When the sap in some trees froze, the trunks burst, making sounds like gunshots. One woman swore she could hear the bark all night, "like cracking walnuts." Fruit that was still on the trees was frozen hard as rock. Blackened groves appeared to have been swept by forest fire. The fruit crop was lost in the first freeze; the trees were lost in the second one. Growers had shipped more than a billion oranges in 1894. In 1895, the number shipped decreased by 97 percent. Vegetable growers who had been preparing to harvest crops were wiped out, too. Bank closures were common. While many immigrant growers left the country, countless American growers fled Florida for other states. Some English citizens moved to the Bahamas.

As one farmer put it: "The beauty is all gone from Florida. . . . We are almost stunned by the magnitude of the calamity." It was not unusual to see homes abandoned, some with the doors left wide open, prepared food still on the table. There were reports of suicides. Newspaper headlines in Tampa's *Times-Union* screamed, "Dead. Everything Is Dead."

Even the railroads were not immune to the effects of the freeze. Before the disaster more than five and a half million crates of citrus were shipped by rail. After it, fewer than 200,000 crates moved over the rails.

Florida had experienced freezes before, but they had never been so devastating, since early on there were fewer groves. As times became more prosperous, more settlers arrived in the area. New farmers and old did well, investing more and more of their energy and resources in the land, mainly in citrus. Then came this, the worst disaster ever in modern Central Florida.

The Florida Commissioner of Agriculture, L. B. Wombell, reported that in a single night "fifty million dollars worth of Florida's most valuable property disappeared." Dispirited and depressed, many growers lost their entire income. At that time there was no help from the government, no disaster relief, no processing industry to convert frozen oranges to juice.

There were a few exceptions. In Polk County, the town of Keystone City, which was surrounded by lakes and at a slightly higher elevation, survived the freeze to enjoy its newfound reputation as a Garden of Eden in the midst of a barren wilderness. Keystone City enjoyed its new fame so much, its people changed the name of their town to Frostproof.

One farmer in Pinellas County, who owned property near the tip of the peninsula that was surrounded on three sides by water and warmed by breezes from the Gulf of Mexico, said his crops weren't affected at all. Ordinarily, he collected $1.50 for a crate of his citrus, but after the freeze he had no misgivings about charging $15.00 a crate.

On the other side of the state, Henry A. DeLand, though not a grower, found himself in much the same circumstances as the citrus growers. Having poured most of his considerable personal fortune into founding his town, he was faced with making good on the guarantees of excellent crop yields and the grand promises he had made to investors who were now disillusioned and wanted out. A man of his word, he honored his pledges, but in the process he was financially ruined.

Devastating though the "Great Citrus Freeze" was for farmers and growers, its effects were felt throughout Florida. Orlando recorded a drop in population, the only time such a thing ever happened in her history. Tampa reported citizens complaining about the large numbers of drifters and beggars, the logical result of having 2,000 men out of jobs. Citrus growing transferred to the southern part of the state, taking people, including growers, bankers, doctors, and shopkeepers, along with it. Citrus production increased so much in the Pinellas-Hillsborough area, due to the surge of citrus farmers, that it split to form two separate counties.

Some small towns turned into ghost towns, never to be mentioned again. At the Florida State Horticultural Society, a speaker said, "It is doubtful if any single industry, in any state, has ever sustained so great a loss, but it has not been destroyed, nor will it be."

Julia Tuttle, a major property owner in Miami who was often referred to as the "Mother of Miami," saw the Great Freeze as a golden opportunity. Julia, a young widow who envisioned the small settlement she lived in one day becoming "the most important port on the Atlantic Coast in the South," knew that dream would never come true without adequate transportation to bring settlers and tourists to the area. With that in mind she had been trying to convince multimillionaire Henry Flagler to extend his railroad from its terminal in Palm Beach to the southern tip of the peninsula. Again and again he had refused. When the Great Freeze sent vacationers scurrying north, even leaving his fabulous Palm Beach hotel, Julia seized the opportunity to send him some orange blossoms from her Miami trees. Flagler, a man of action, was on a launch headed south the following day. When he reached Miami three days later, he bowed to Julia, announcing, "I am Henry Flagler and these must be the shores of paradise."

He extended his railroad to "paradise," starting the first passenger train service to Miami in 1896, although he stubbornly continued to maintain that, "the town [Miami] will never be more than a fishing village for my hotel guests." As word about the railroad got out, many of the citrus-connected people who had been ruined followed him, hoping for desperately needed work. Others held fast in the northern part of the state, where farmers varied their vegetable crops and cattle ranching grew in importance.

Henry DeLand, his confidence badly shaken, had had enough. With a heavy heart, he settled his affairs in Volusia County, turning over his responsibilities at Stetson University to his friend, John Stetson. DeLand returned to his old home in Fairport, New York, restarting his manufacturing business, and living quietly and more humbly to the end of his days. When he died, his debts had all been repaid.

After the Great Freeze farmers who remained in Central Florida began to find success in diversification. Cattle ranching, always a major industry, continued to expand. More dairies were established. Citrus made a slow comeback, shifting farther south. The replanting process for citrus trees in Florida is a lengthy one, the trees being classified as nonbearing for the first four years. It was not until 1911–1912 that the first really good Florida citrus crop became available again, but when it did, the word spread.

After the 1895 freeze, the U.S. Weather Service in Jacksonville greatly improved its system of providing severe cold warnings. It sent telegrams to one hundred offices, then those offices sent notices to other offices, and so on, spreading the alert. The railroads were also enlisted to use a certain whistle that was an announcement of imminent cold weather to growers in rural areas. Forewarned, citrus growers were then able to use controlled fire to save their groves.

The Sunshine State was recovering and tourists began returning to the area. As usual, Florida did what she excels at—she bounced back.

CHAPTER 5

CRANE'S OPEN BOAT

The Wreck of the Filibustering *Commodore*

1897

Americans have always had great compassion for the people in other countries who revolted against oppression. So it was in 1895, when Cuban insurgents rose up against their hated Spanish rulers, that many Americans, further galvanized by the "yellow journalism" of the Pulitzer and Hearst newspapers, joined in calling for "Cuba Libre!" Cuba's Floridian neighbors, who lived just 90 miles away, were especially eager to offer their assistance, but President Grover Cleveland and, later, President William McKinley steadfastly refused to allow the United States to get involved. (Secretary of the Navy Theodore Roosevelt, who was eager to join the action, would complain that his boss, President McKinley, "had the backbone of a chocolate eclair.")

The Cuban revolutionaries, badly in need of supplies, enlisted the help of sympathetic Americans who were willing to engage in filibustering arms and ammunition to Cuba, even though gunrunning was illegal. Filibustering was exciting and adventurous, and besides that the pay was good—so good that a number of tugboats seen frequently in Jacksonville's harbor made so many runs, they came to be known as "the Cuban Fleet." One of them, *Three Friends,* belonged to the future Florida governor, Napoleon Bonaparte Broward. Although *Three Friends* was built for towing and carrying freight from Jacksonville to the Bahamas, she was also implicated in several filibustering expeditions.

The fate of another steamer had to be on the minds of anyone involved in smuggling supplies to the Cuban rebels. In 1873 the U.S. ship *Virginius* was sailing from New York on a filibustering expedition but was seized by a Spanish cruiser and taken to Cuba where her captain and fifty-three of her crew were shot before a firing squad. It was after that episode that the U.S. government declared filibustering illegal and all future activities were done in secret, with the vessel's name and any other identifying marks removed.

Another ship of the "Cuban Fleet" was the *Commodore,* a 178-ton steamship, which was built in Philadelphia in 1882, with its home base in New York. According to her former chief engineer, the *Commodore* was by far the best of the filibustering fleet, "staunch and seaworthy, fit for any weather and strong enough to sink an ordinary iron steamer." Built of wood, with a single coal-fired engine, she was 123 feet long and 19 feet in her beam and had a crew of twenty-eight or twenty-nine men, including some Cubans, under the leadership of Paul Rojo, who were anxious to join the action at home.

One of the crew, a twenty-eight-year-old man who had signed on as Samuel Carleton, was in reality a celebrity whose real name was Stephen Crane. He was the author of *The Red Badge of Courage,* a Civil War novel considered by many to be a masterpiece. Crane was working undercover for the *New York Press* and was assigned to report on the events in Cuba.

When he arrived in Jacksonville, the leading U.S. filibustering port, he registered at the St. James, the city's most elegant 500-room hotel, most likely a benefit of his expense account. One of the people he met in the hotel dining room was Captain Edward Murphy, who had been gunrunning with the *Commodore* for some time. "Samuel Carleton" signed on as an able seaman at twenty dollars a month.

The *Commodore* had already made several illegal trips to Cuba but had also been turned back twice by the U.S. government's revenue cutters. This time, the filibustering trip was open and above board due to a recent ruling by the U. S. attorney general that shipping arms to Cuba was not illegal. So open was the loading of the ship in broad daylight, Crane noted that it was "as if she were going to carry oranges to New York, instead of Remingtons to Cuba."

Because there was still much red tape to attend to before officials reluctantly gave permission for the trip, it was sunset before Captain Murphy returned to the *Commodore* and the crew made ready to depart. Finally, with three long, mournful blasts of her horn, the *Commodore* slipped away from her dock and headed for the Cuban port of Cienfuegas, about 1,500 miles away. Cubans on shore cheered as she passed by, carrying supplies to sustain their revolution.

At its mouth the St. Johns River twists and turns and at that time was shaded by huge live oaks with hanging vines. The sun set early on New Year's Eve, so the darkness combined with a blanket of fog to make visibility difficult, even for the river pilot, Tom Smith. Despite his familiarity with the area, the *Commodore* had gone less than 2 miles out of Jacksonville in the intense fog before she was grounded on a mudflat, which carried the prescient name, Commodore's Point. Captain Murphy elected to remain in that rather humiliating position until morning when the revenue cutter *Boutwell* came to their assistance, hauling the ship from the mud on New Year's Day. The *Commodore* was under way again—but not for long. Incredibly, she grounded again in the winding channel of the St. Johns River, but as the *Boutwell* advanced on her once more, the captain reversed her engines and freed the tanker. Undoubtedly, all aboard must have felt a great sense of relief at being under way again, heading for open sea.

The relief wouldn't have lasted long, however, for as soon as the *Commodore* left the inlet at 2:00 p.m., she was greeted with heavy rollers that turned into huge black waves. As night began to fall, a nasty southeast squall whipped through. In short order many of the men were seasick.

The amateur seaman, Stephen Crane, felt fine as he roamed through the ship, trying to learn as much as he could for his assignment. In the galley he chatted for a long time with the cook, Charles B. Montgomery, who confessed to having had a premonition that something bad would happen to the *Commodore*. Montgomery added though, that he felt sure they would come through with whatever fate had in store for them.

Not unduly alarmed, Crane made his way through the lurching ship to the pilot house to talk with the helmsman, Tom Smith. Smith, a veteran of many rough voyages, said this one would be his last. The pay was good, he said, but he decided it was time to retire.

Crane continued his rounds through the ship, but no sooner had he begun talking with the captain, than the engineer, James Rodigan, stumbled into the pilot house to report there were several inches of water in the boiler room. Not only that, the pumps were down and he couldn't get rid of the water. There was no suction, probably because water had gotten to the coal, washed it into the pipes, and evidently choked the pipe to the pumps.

The captain calmly ordered Rodigan to return to the boiler room and get the men started on a bucket brigade. He had other men stoke the furnace to capacity in an attempt to generate enough steam to reach Mosquito Inlet, 18 miles away. He next alerted the Cuban leader, Paul Rojo, to get his men to work with buckets, too. Stephen Crane joined them in the hold of the ship. The oiler, a young sailor named Billy Higgins, led them all in filling buckets with water from the bilge, passing them along a line of men who handed them up and dumped them over the side. It seemed a hopeless job, though, as the men watched the water level slowly rise. They were unable to keep up with it. The ship had proceeded only 3 miles when the water level reached the boiler and doused the fire.

The heat, the water roiling around, the noise, the darkness, the slamming of the men against the sides of the ship and against each other from the powerful waves—all prompted Crane to later compare it to "the middle kitchen of hades."

By 3:00 a.m. everyone knew it was hopeless. Captain Murphy ordered the anchor lowered in an attempt to keep the ship's bow into the waves, then he called for the men to loosen the lifeboats and prepare to launch them. Some of the Cubans, not very experienced seamen, started lowering a lifeboat, but it swung away, out of their control, and knocked the captain to the deck, badly injuring his arm.

They managed to launch the first boat with twelve Cuban men aboard and that boat reached the shore near the Mosquito Inlet Lighthouse at about 10:00 a.m. The second boat with six Cubans reached the shore at noon near Port Orange. The captain, who had somehow succeeded in getting his arm into a sling, ordered Crane to prepare to launch the 10-foot dinghy in the forward part of the ship. When it was in the water, Captain Murphy, Montgomery, and Crane climbed into it and shoved away from the tug with the captain holding one end of a line that was fastened to the ship's rail. The captain was determined to remain beside the *Commodore* until he was sure she was sinking. With the first light of dawn, a shocking sight greeted them. They thought they were the last to leave the ship but standing at the rail of the *Commodore* was a group of men, waving frantically.

As it happened, the third lifeboat that was launched, with seven Americans aboard, had been hit by a violent wave, smashed against the ship's hull, and sank. The men, including First Mate Frank Grane, managed to climb back aboard the *Commodore* and frantically tie three makeshift rafts together. Three men were able to save themselves using the rafts, but Frank Grane was not one of the lucky ones. He leaped overboard, apparently preferring suicide to whatever horror awaited.

One of the men on a raft tossed a line to the dinghy, which Montgomery grabbed, attempting to pull the raft along. All at once, their dinghy was going backward, and they realized that one man on the raft was hysterically pulling the line, apparently trying to reach the dinghy with the idea of boarding it. The dinghy was already dangerously overloaded, having a mere six inches of gunwale between its occupants and the raging sea. Montgomery had no choice; he let go of the line just as the *Commodore* suddenly started to sink. The rafts were gone, with all the men on them. The dinghy barely got away in time.

So began what would be a long test of the four men left in the dinghy. Crane, Montgomery, and Higgins took turns bailing water from the crowded little boat, the captain being disabled with his broken arm. He gave them directions, trying to guide them to reach the lighthouse, but the stormy sea made steering and rowing unbelievably difficult. After a while Crane fastened his coat to an oar and hoisted it up to act as a sail, in that way conserving at least some of their energy.

A shark seemed to appreciate their precarious condition, persistently following their dinghy, even bumping the side of it, possibly hoping to upset them. Cold, wet, hungry, and fatigued, they spent thirty grueling hours in the little dinghy, until finally the captain could see the men were nearly exhausted and wouldn't be able to hold on much longer. He ordered them to get as close to shore as they possibly could before the enormous breakers upset them.

At one point, they saw a man on shore and tried to attract his attention by waving a towel they had fished out of the water but it was as though they were invisible. The man simply walked away.

It was getting light again when a huge wave knocked them all into the icy sea. Crane wriggled out of some of the heavy clothes that weighed him down, dumped a pouch containing $700 into the ocean, and tried to swim through a powerful riptide for the shore.

This time they were lucky. A citizen from Daytona, John Kitchell, was walking on the beach when he spotted them. Peeling off his clothes, he swam to them and pulled them to safety, one at a time, except for Billy Higgins. Higgins had hit his head when they were launching the dinghy and probably no one realized how badly he was hurt at the time. Kitchell made a valiant effort to save him, but Higgins was dead.

Suddenly, people appeared from out of nowhere, with blankets, hot coffee, and flasks. The ordeal was over.

Montgomery would later talk about his premonition and there were persistent rumors of sabotage, but none was ever proven.

Stephen Crane died in 1900 of tuberculosis, thought by some to have been brought on by his thirty hours in the icy ocean. Before he died, he wrote a short story, "The Open Boat," a fictional tale about his shipwreck experience. The story, frequently anthologized, is considered to be one of the finest short stories ever written in the English language.

CHAPTER 6

A CITY IN FLAMES

The Jacksonville Fire
1901

Jacksonville celebrated the new century by basking in prosperity. The city of 30,000 had entertained 15,000 visitors during the winter season and was looking forward to more of the same with the imminent opening of Henry Flagler's grand new hotel. Then, too, one of Jacksonville's favorite sons had recently been elected to the state legislature and his hometown expected great things from Napoleon Bonaparte Broward. Having rebounded from the disastrous yellow fever epidemic of 1888, expectations for the city's future were high.

There had been no rain for more than a month, and although the air was sultry on Friday, May 3, 1901, there was no wind and the sky was a gorgeous blue. Some workers at the Cleveland Fibre Factory were enjoying lunch outdoors near a platform where Spanish moss had been spread out to dry. The aroma of food being prepared on a wood stove in a nearby shanty floated through the air. It was unfortunately accompanied by some sparks drifting along with it, instantly igniting the moss. Smoke from the moss caught the attention of the workers who scrambled about, trying to douse small, scattered fires with buckets of water. But from out of nowhere, a brisk wind picked up burning

Looking west at Jacksonville homes on fire.
FLORIDA PHOTOGRAPHIC COLLECTION/FLORIDA STATE ARCHIVES

fibers, wafting them to the warehouse, a building constructed of pitch pine with a roof of combustible shingles and packed full of moss. With a thunderous crash the factory roof caved in, allowing more burning fibers to rise, float over neighboring buildings, scatter onto more roofs, and enter open windows and ignite curtains. Horrified to see the fire spreading so rapidly, the workers summoned the fire department, which arrived quickly and fought valiantly, but Fire Chief Thomas W. Haney quickly realized they had almost no chance of containing it. Telegrams pleading for help brought firefighters from Brunswick, Waycross, and Savannah, Georgia, and from Fernandina and St. Augustine. By that time a wall of flames a half-mile wide roared like a monster, through the streets, heading east, devouring everything in its path.

Jacksonville residents did not immediately appreciate the serious-ness of their situation, thinking if they were carried their valuables and household goods a few blocks to the east, they would be safe until the fire was extinguished. But as the showers of flames fell from the sky and the fire leaped across four, sometimes five buildings at a time, distraught families packed their belongings into wagons and tried to escape. Some streets were impassable, the heat in others intolerable, still other streets were filled with crowds, panicked horses, and shrieking people dumping their belongings and heading for the river.

It was a splendid day in Tallahassee. When the House of Representatives paused for lunch, Representative Napoleon Bonaparte Broward walked past the Western Union office on his way through town. An excited telegraph operator gave him the news about his hometown that had come over the wire. Not only was Broward concerned about his constituents, but he was also worried about his Jacksonville home, which was being cared for by his father-in-law while the Broward family lived in the state capitol during his term in office.

When Governor William S. Jennings dispatched a special train of troops to help Jacksonville with rescue work and in keeping order, Broward received permission to go along. Every time the train stopped to take on more water, Broward hopped off to check the Jacksonville news with Western Union. It was never comforting.

By 3:20 that afternoon, the Windsor Hotel, where many people fled with their belongings, was burning. A reporter later wrote, "The burning of a hotel like the Windsor would ordinarily be regarded as a disaster in itself, but yesterday it lapsed into relative insignificance." Refugees barely had time to escape from the building, most without any of their belongings. Minutes later, the St. James Hotel, which had closed for the end of the season, was enveloped in flames.

Another reporter noted: "All in a moment a blinding typhoon of smoke and dust came with overwhelming power, blowing eastward, and it was necessary for those in the street to run to escape it. For a time it seemed that the fierce advance was straight to the east. House after house succumbed. No effort was made to save buildings now.

Everyone knew that to save any building in the track of the fury was impossible, and on and on it sped. Churches, public buildings, and shops were destroyed."

Destroyed along with innumerable houses were the two hotels, churches and synagogues, schools, offices, city hall, police and fire stations, and the armory, where people went for safety, crumbled "like an eggshell," with huge amounts of valuables inside. The courthouse, a sturdy redbrick structure, was another place people felt it was safe to take valuable belongings. It did hold up until the building next door caught on fire, and shortly thereafter, the courthouse glowed brilliantly and the roof fell in. The walls remained, but everything inside was gone. The Hubbard building was cause for intense concern because of the dynamite and gunpowder stored inside, making life even more difficult for firemen.

On the packed streets bricklike cypress paving blocks buckled, concrete glowed red, and buildings crumbled. It was feared the docks and highly valued waterfront would be destroyed, but a superhuman effort on the part of firemen saved it.

Haunted by memories of the recent yellow fever epidemic, some people believed this latest disaster to befall their city must mean that for some reason, the Lord was angry with Jacksonville. They prepared to die. Others rose to the occasion as never before. One able-bodied man was hurrying through the streets clutching his valuables when he spotted an elderly couple struggling along, further burdened by a heavy sewing machine. When he called out to them to drop the machine and run for their lives, the woman tearfully answered, "How can I, Sir? This machine is the only support of my poor old husband." The younger man wordlessly dropped his belongings, shouldered the sewing machine, and led the couple to safety.

People whose homes escaped the conflagration opened their homes to strangers who were not so lucky. Men and boys formed bucket brigades, helping to save some homes. Strong young men

Downtown building in flames.
FLORIDA PHOTOGRAPHIC COLLECTION/FLORIDA STATE ARCHIVES

carried sick people to safety, only to have to carry them to another location when the flames advanced again. Women beat out the flames for each other when their long dresses caught fire. One young woman had her hat yanked from her head, but she was assured it was on fire when she looked questioningly at the perpetrator.

At the Market Street Bridge, some people leaped into the water, figuring they would be safe there. When a rumor spread that the gasworks that was only a block away was about to explode, the swimmers must have thought the end was near. The rumor soon proved to be false.

In the meantime Representative Broward, having observed his fellow citizens from the train window as his train traveled parallel to a highway, prepared himself for the worst. As the train crept along, he could see the destruction and the sad condition of his people through the smoke and dust. On arriving in Jacksonville he was surprised to find his family home intact, thanks to his father-in-law who had saved it by using wet blankets to douse falling sparks. Broward immediately began helping in whatever capacity he was needed, later helping to found the Jacksonville Relief Association and generously donating many family linens and household goods to people who'd lost everything. He formed plans to introduce bills to the legislature to rebuild schools and provide for other improvements, and he hurried back to Tallahassee two days later ready to do just that.

At 8:30 that night, the fire department announced the fire was under control. People camped for the night wherever they could find a place—in vacant lots, under trees, on the floors of strangers' houses that had been spared. Everything—food, water, space—was shared.

On Saturday morning a meeting was called to order. There was no time to waste in getting started on formal relief measures, with the help of some people who had been active in the yellow fever epidemic a few years earlier and whose expertise was valuable. On Sunday the Jacksonville Relief Association was officially organized. The first order of business was to send out a report on the situation in Jacksonville and to seek help. Their appeal brought a generous response with donations of food, clothing, tools, cash, and even sewing machines. Western Union sent messages for the association free of charge.

On May 12, H. L. Mencken, a young reporter from the *Baltimore Morning Herald*, arrived to see what was left of Jacksonville. He would later become a world-famous writer, but in 1901 he was a green reporter who had been sent by his editor to cover the story of the fire and also to try to find out what had happened to the two carloads of relief supplies the *Baltimore Morning Herald* had collected and sent to Jacksonville. Supplies were said to include one hundred second-hand horse blankets, ether, whiskey, wooden legs, and coffins. The exhausted young man spent the first night in town sleeping under a piano in a hotel lobby, having found the few available rooms "occupied by newspaper reporters . . . insurance adjusters, brick and lumber salesmen and agents for sprinkling systems and fire extinguishers." He fell asleep quickly but was rudely awakened at 3:00 a.m. by youthful soldiers guarding a bank across the street. One young soldier, thinking he saw an interloper in the bank, fired a machine gun. Mencken confused by sleep, jumped up, banged his head on the sounding board of the piano, and "got a bump that stuck to me until I was back in Baltimore." Mencken recovered nicely with vinegar and butcher paper first aid from the hotel night clerk. He was gratified to learn that about a third of the people being fed by the Jacksonville Relief Association were given rations supplied by Baltimore.

In order to distribute supplies efficiently, eleven commissaries were formed in various sections of the city, feeding from ten to twelve thousand people daily. They also distributed bedding, clothing, household necessities, and tools. As the cleanup progressed, people who were out of work were employed to clean 22 miles of streets, repair sewers, and cut thousands of blackened tree stumps. Dead animals were removed and disposed of along with other debris. The federal government supplied twelve thousand tents so that before long all homeless residents were at least temporarily sheltered.

Soon after the Relief Association came into being, women formed an auxiliary to supplement the men's work. Their bureau of information invited all women to come and simply ask for whatever they needed, promising that the auxiliary would provide it. They found themselves dispensing food, supplies, medicines, and even providing nurses when necessary. They set up a sewing tent, hiring women to sew badly needed bedding and other household articles.

To match the rapidity with which the fire swept away so much of Jacksonville, her citizens made a determined recovery from what was recorded as the largest metropolitan fire in the South. In eight hours the fire burned 466 acres, 23 churches, 10 hotels, 8,677 homes, 146 city blocks, 2,368 buildings, and all public records. Miraculously, just seven people had perished. Property damage was estimated at fifteen million dollars, of which one-third was covered by insurance. The glare from the fire was visible in Savannah; spirals of smoke could be seen in Raleigh, North Carolina.

As he walked through part of the city, H. L. Mencken summarized his feelings in this way: "Today the ruins stand like Pompeii— tall spires of crumbling brick and hillocks of cracked and powdered stone. Ordinarily a burned house appears as a smoky shell with black and damp interior. But in the ruins in Jacksonville there is no trace of black, for the fire burned everything that was burnable, and when it was gone and its work was done, there remain but white ashes and swirling dust. In the place of these white ashes and stumps of walls there stood, 10 days ago, about $15,000,000 worth of houses. Today they are worth 10 cents a carload, delivered at the dump."

Although the city was recovering nicely, when agitators from Tampa arrived in town to stir up labor unrest, the patience of Jacksonville's citizens was depleted. The rabble-rousers were promptly run out of town.

Jacksonville citizens liked to say, on Friday they had a fire, on Saturday they recovered, on Sunday they worshiped, and on Monday they issued the first building permit for the reconstruction of their city. Jacksonville would rebuild and the city would be even better than it was before.

CHAPTER 7

"LYNCH LAW WILL PREVAIL"

The Destruction of Rosewood

1923

In 1923 the total destruction of an entire black community, including the confirmed deaths of at least eight but possibly more of its citizens, plus the wounding or injuring of an untold number of others, took place in the land of the free and home of the brave.

Rosewood, a small village about 9 miles east of Cedar Key, on Florida's west coast, was home to twenty-five to thirty mostly black families, along with three churches, a general store, a baseball diamond, a train station, some single-room cabins, and a small school building that also housed the black Masonic hall. The town was named for the plentiful huge red cedar trees that grew in the area and had pale, rose-colored wood.

Cedarwood was used for the manufacture of lead pencils. After being cut in Rosewood, it was shipped by rail to two large pencil companies in Cedar Key, then on to New York. By 1890, when all the cedar trees in Rosewood had been harvested, white families had moved away, selling their properties to the remaining black families. Sumner, a white hamlet 3 miles to the west, was where many Rosewood men were employed in the Cummer and Sons Cypress Mill, and where some of their wives worked in the white households. Other black men had jobs at a black-owned Rosewood company that distilled turpentine and rosin from the abundant pine trees in the area. Blacks also worked in a turpentine still in Wylly, a mile to the east.

It was just five years after World War I ended, and returning African-American servicemen who had honorably served their country rightfully anticipated being welcomed home and accepted as full U.S. citizens. How heartbreaking it must have been to discover that not only had violent racism actually spread in the country they had fought for but that membership of the Ku Klux Klan was by then measured in the millions. Lynchings were not uncommon, especially in the South, and Florida was no exception.

In December 1922 in Perry, a black man was burned at the stake and a church, school, and other buildings were incinerated. On New Year's Eve that same year, the KKK held a rally and parade in nearby Gainesville, described by local newspapers as the "largest crowd in the history of the city." The events that would make Rosewood famous began in neighboring Sumner the next morning, Sunday, January 1, 1923, one of the coldest in people's memory.

Fannie Taylor, a twenty-year-old married woman, mother of two small children, and wife of James Taylor, age thirty, was home after her husband went to work at the sawmill in Sumner. Most of the town was still asleep when Taylor arrived at his mill job, which was to oil the equipment and have it ready before the other workers arrived. Taylor then routinely returned home for breakfast before heading back to the mill for the rest of the day. This day, however, would be very different.

While Taylor was oiling machinery, his wife burst through the front door of their home and stood on the porch, screaming hysterically, her face bruised and bleeding. Women in the neighborhood heard her, rushed to help, and were horrified when Fannie told them how she had answered a knock on her door and a black man had forced his way into the house and attacked her. Terrified for her children, she wept uncontrollably while the women led her to a neighbor's home. Some of the women returned to the Taylor house, finding no one there except the little ones, who were unharmed. The women brought the children to the neighbor's home, where they had helped Fannie to lie down. Some cared for her and some for the children, while an angry mob who heard the commotion formed outside and rumors spread like wildfire.

A summary of the attack's extent depended on the color of the person talking about it. Whites characterized it as rape; blacks did not. But gradually the ugly tale spread that Fannie Taylor had been attacked by a black man. When her husband arrived home, the sheriff was there, and the gathering crowd had been informed that a black convict named Jesse Hunter had escaped from a working road gang the day before and was already being pursued by bloodhounds. The hounds smelled Fannie's clothing and headed straight for Rosewood, closely followed by a pack of white men, mostly armed and all very angry.

The dogs led the rowdy mob to the home of a black veteran, Aaron Carrier, but the house seemed empty, and there was no response to the furious crowd's demands for him. Convinced that Carrier must have helped Hunter escape, the mob moved on to the nearby home of Aaron's mother, Emma Carrier, shouting for her son.

Blocking the door, Emma yelled out at them that her son was sick and had been there in bed for days. "He done nothing wrong!" she screamed over and over, but they shoved her aside, entered the home, and pulled Aaron from his bed and away from the house. They tied him to the bumper of a car and dragged him over the road until, in pain and fear, he begged for mercy, claiming the man they wanted was Sam Carter, a local blacksmith.

The escalating situation would have led to a lynching, but Levy County Sheriff Bob Walker stepped in and removed Carrier to the safety of the Alachua County Jail in Gainesville, while fifty or so angry white men swarmed over the small, isolated Carter house at the town's border. Determined to learn the whereabouts of Jesse Hunter from him, they hid until Carter arrived home on his wagon, grabbed him, and demanded answers.

When he did not respond fast enough, the mob tied a rope around his neck, looped it over a nearby tree limb, and lifted his body partway off the ground. Carter writhed and jerked in agony until they lowered him to the ground, took out their knives, and began hacking off body parts—ears, fingers, genitals—to be kept in jars as keepsakes. Then one of the attackers shot Carter in the face. The mob hung the bloody, mutilated body from a tree, riddled it with bullets, and left it as a warning to other black residents.

Emotions ran high among the whites of Sumner, inflamed by the knowledge that Fannie Taylor's attacker had not been caught. But Fannie's account of the day's events was not the same account that would be given in the future by Sarah Carrier and her granddaughter Philomena, who were at Fannie's house that horrible day.

Sarah, who was hired to do Fannie's weekly laundry and ironing, had been questioned by authorities and, fearing the others, said she saw nothing. But later she told neighbors that the man Fannie claimed not to have known was really her lover, a white railroad worker who visited her often when Sarah was there working and James was not at home. That day the lovers had apparently quarreled and the boyfriend had roughed up Fannie before he left. In a desperate cover-up, Fannie lied about a black attacker to her neighbors and to her husband.

Some of the blacks in Rosewood hoped the ugliness and killing were over and would not be repeated, but angered whites in Sumner believed Fannie's story. A posse of four or five hundred men, many of them intoxicated, relentlessly looked for Jesse Hunter, and for blood . . . in Rosewood.

Sylvester Carrier, a cousin of Aaron Carrier and Sarah's son, did not believe the evil was past. A tall, well-dressed black man, Sylvester stood out wherever he went, especially at the Methodist church, where he played the organ and sang solos with the choir, and at his home, where he gave lessons on the family piano. Working as a fur trapper and giving piano lessons provided a comfortable living for Sylvester, who supported his wife, mother, and three sisters.

Sylvester, a proud man who was considered uppity by many Sumner whites, assumed himself to be the family defender. As tensions mounted, he rounded up fifteen to twenty-five relatives and hustled them all to his mother's large house on two pleasant acres of land, where he felt it would be easier to mount a defense. A few neighborhood whites refused to go against the black people who lived nearby, and Sylvester had help from about twelve other black men scattered about the area, mostly Mason pals who were also war veterans, armed and ready for trouble.

When the mob arrived at Sarah's porch, they yelled for the women and children to come out so they'd not get hurt, saying they only wanted to ask Sylvester about Jesse Hunter. Sarah, who had nursed and cared for some of the white men when they were children, raised a window and shouted at them to go home, as though they were still her charges. Instantly, gunshot pierced the air, glass shattered, and Sarah fell dead.

The quiet night exploded. Sylvester's friends, hidden in the surrounding woods, started shooting, while Sylvester calmly waited inside with two guns aimed at the front door. When two members of the mob opened the front door, Sylvester shot twice, killing them both. Another of the mob who approached the house was shot in the head.

As word of the battle spread, more whites arrived and an onslaught ensued. The women inside tried to protect the children on the second floor until about four in the morning, when the mob retreated to wait for dawn. The survivors left the house and hid in the woods. The mob returned at daylight to find bloody devastation and the bodies of

Sylvester and his mother. There was no stopping the mayhem—everything in sight was smashed and destroyed before it was set on fire.

Crowds kept coming, from Jacksonville and even as far as Georgia, and the devastation went on. Many black residents fled or went into hiding, but there would be more black victims. Lexie Gordon, fearing for her two grown daughters, had sent them to safety, but she was too weak from typhoid fever to leave her home. When the horde set the house on fire, she staggered from her bed, attempting to escape. Shot instantly, she became victim number six.

Sarah's elderly brother-in-law, James Carrier, had survived the melee. On Saturday he was walking toward Sumner, intending to search for a daughter who lived there. Suddenly he was captured, dragged to the graves in a Rosewood cemetery, and questioned about Jesse Hunter's whereabouts. The brave grandfather refused to answer and, despite having just one arm, was forced to dig his own grave. The whites finally shot him in the head and left his body there.

Eventually there were no more homes of blacks in Rosewood left to burn. It had taken only seven days to wipe out the entire village. The editor of the *Gainesville Daily Sun,* an acknowledged KKK member, expressed his horror in a published column. However, he ended the piece by saying, "Law or no law, courts or no courts—as long as criminal assaults on innocent women continue, lynch law will prevail, and blood will be shed."

The disaster lasted just one week, and Rosewood was no more.

CHAPTER 8

A FLOATING HOTEL SINKS

The Capsize of the *Prinz Valdemar*
1926

As early as 1925 some business authorities in the North were heard suggesting that Miami's extraordinary building boom of the Roaring Twenties had crested. Miamians, and the outsiders who flocked there in the early 1920s, blissfully ignored the warnings, continuing to buy up land and sell it for such spectacular profits; it seemed downright foolish not to get involved. Everything was a "steal," so why not take advantage? This was a genuine boom and everyone wanted a piece of it.

Many factors contributed to making South Florida real estate attractive. Aside from the fantastic climate, few could ignore the fact that there was no state income and no inheritance tax, details the 5,917 working real estate agents in Miami would not let anyone forget. All this was touted on the pages of the *Miami Herald,* which contributed to the paper's enormous advertising space, more in 1925 than any other paper in the world. The *St. Petersburg Times* was a close second, with newspaper ads and the boom feeding off each other. When the news that a university would be built in Coral Gables was released, people who had been concerned about the legitimacy of the building boom became convinced they should participate in it.

Florida railroads were so swamped carrying materials for the construction of hotels, skyscrapers, and other buildings, the Florida East Coast Railroad was forced to declare an embargo on almost everything except food. Not only was there was a dire lack of storage space for the 2,200 railroad cars that were waiting to be unloaded, the FECR needed to take some time to repair the wear and tear on their overused tracks. As a result shortages were common in nearly everything but especially in lumber and bricks, glass and doorknobs, and all kinds of items needed to finish the hotels, houses, and office buildings that were half-completed. Since the railroads continued to ship food, crafty suppliers sometimes transported bags of cement or other construction items in refrigerated cars as though they were perishable. One builder admitted he shipped a carload of bricks by piling tons of ice around the bricks and marking the car with signs that read LETTUCE. Builders hired guards to prevent highjacking of materials.

Some rundown northern ships that had been designated to be demolished were temporarily resurrected and overhauled just enough to enable them to make a final trip to Miami, hauling precious construction materials. The material they hauled was worth more than the resurrected ships, and their captains were under orders to ditch the bedraggled vessels after they emptied their cargoes in Florida. The always busy Miami harbor became increasingly congested, vessels having to wait interminably for dockage while they anchored offshore, and there were more ships on the way. As if that weren't enough, the citrus crop that year was a bumper crop, requiring quick shipments north when the harbor was jammed.

Opportunistic dock workers seized the moment to go on strike, demanding a 15-cent raise, to 60 cents an hour. Following in their footsteps, 1,800 telegraphers struck, thoroughly interfering with communications.

Adding to the mayhem, the highways were jammed with northerners coming in automobiles to seek their fortunes, even in the

Capsized *Prinz Valdemar* blocking Miami Harbor.
FLORIDA PHOTOGRAPHIC COLLECTION/FLORIDA STATE ARCHIVES

summer, whereas in the past there had been a definite slump in warmer months. The resulting dire shortage of rooms forced many people to sleep in their cars, on beaches, or in parks. Old barges, derelict yachts, almost anything that floated was tied to a dock and rented for sleeping accommodations.

In a move to help alleviate the lodging shortage, a group of developers purchased an old Danish warship in New York, the barkentine *Prinz Valdemar,* that had long been used as a training vessel. With the idea of converting her into a hundred-room floating hotel, they took on a cargo of building material and headed her south. Defying the odds, she and her crew survived gale winds that sank some other ships on the way. The *Prinz Valdemar* was huge—241 feet with four tall masts, the largest sailing ship to ever try entering the crowded harbor in Miami. River pilots thought it best to keep her sitting outside the harbor for a week until the seas were absolutely calm. The crew and building mechanics, eighty in all, watched and waited until January 10, 1926, when conditions seemed favorable.

The channel was just eighteen feet deep but even with all her ballast removed, the *Prinz Valdemar* went aground on a sandbar as she was being towed into the turning basin. Her four huge masts towering above her empty hull made the ship exceedingly top heavy. The tide went out at the same moment that a strong northeast wind picked up the empty ship and she started toppling over sideways. The surprised crew scrambled up on deck, rushed to the port side of the ship, hoping their collective weight would prevent her from keeling over any farther to the starboard side. As she continued tilting, the captain ordered two men on shore to try to fasten lines from the ship to pilings on the dock in an attempt to keep her from going down, but the big lines were too heavy for the two men to handle and they were unsuccessful.

Frustration followed frustration as radio messages to the Coast Guard and other dispatches to a passing tug went unanswered. Nothing seemed to be working, but in the four minutes it took for the ship to tilt over, eighty men had sufficient time to jump overboard. All survived thanks to a Coast Guard cutter that reached the area, pulled the men from the water, and supplied them with dry clothes before hauling them to shore.

A poker game had been under way on the lower deck and among the players was a steward who had just left the game to attend to some of his duties. It was he who alerted the other men, but before they could do anything, water started flooding in under the table where they were playing. They all scrambled to the upper side of the wet, slippery vessel and jumped overboard. One man reached shore clutching dice and the last pot from the game. "I guess I won it," he said.

The last to leave the ship were two Japanese cooks who at first were feared to be missing. Later, after everyone thought the ship was empty, someone saw parcels being tossed out of a porthole. Upon investigation, the two cooks were discovered trying to salvage some hams and other supplies from their damaged galley.

There was really nothing that the Coast Guard cutter at the scene could do about the 241-foot ship with 100-foot masts lying on its side across Miami's busy harbor. The port was effectively closed. And closed it remained for nearly a month while everyone tried to figure out what to do. A few people were amused at the absurdity of the situation. More were annoyed. Many more were enraged. It was a financial catastrophe.

Nearly one hundred ships were off shore, waiting to enter Miami's harbor. Between them all, they carried about forty-five million feet of lumber desperately needed by builders to complete construction projects. There were eleven ships, freight steamers, and schooners, emptied of their cargo, inside the harbor waiting to depart Miami. The cruise ship *George Washington* was preparing to cast off, and there were countless passengers impatient to begin their long-awaited holidays.

It was a situation guaranteed to give headaches to the city commissioners who hurriedly met to seek answers and forge plans for removing the 241-foot barricade from the mouth of their usually bustling harbor. Not unexpectedly, it was easier said than done. An attempt was made to move another large ship alongside the *Prinz Valdemar*, lash the two together, then pull the *Prinz Valdemar* to an upright position. It was an effort that failed.

The nightmare escalated with ships clamoring to get out, other ships clamoring to get in, builders clamoring for materials, and nothing happening. City commissioners telegraphed Governor John Martin with an urgent plea to replace the Miami harbor master, whom they declared incompetent. That effort too went nowhere.

The frantic city commissioners also called in the Army Corps of Engineers who immediately set about digging a secondary 80-foot channel around the *Prinz Valdemar*. Two of the dredges on the job

Although it appears ships could pass around the capsized schooner,
the channel was too shallow for most to do so.
FLORIDA PHOTOGRAPHIC COLLECTION/FLORIDA STATE ARCHIVES

struck some reefs and broke down, calling for the use of dynamite
which, not unexpectedly at this point, was unavailable.

There was not much left to try except to remove the ship's 100-
foot masts with acetylene torches so that some smaller ships could
maneuver around and through the narrow channel. Accordingly,
the *Prinz Valdemar* was demasted, and cargo vessels began carefully

working their way around the ship when almost unbelievably, a steamer, the *Lakevort,* ran aground, closing the channel once more. When some overeager freighter captains tried to edge through the mess, they struck reefs and were themselves grounded.

While all this was going on—or not going on—the crews of the unintentionally idled ships were having vacations of sorts, fishing and sunbathing as they awaited some sort of resolution to the situation. The *Queen of Nassau,* a former Canadian training ship purchased by landowner Barron Collier, anchored nearby to house the crew and workers of the *Prinz Valdemar.* The vessel had been upgraded with the intention of using it for interisland cruises, so the men from the *Prinz Valdemar* most likely enjoyed their forced vacation. In an attempt to make up for the loss of all their personal effects, they were even entertained in the evening by the cast that had been assembled for the floating hotel.

The comedy of errors amused no one remotely involved in it. It was a financial disaster, as desperately needed supplies were so close but unavailable to the firms that needed them, unfinished structures stayed unfinished, construction firms defaulted, subcontractors were unpaid, hotel owners and developers failed, banks wavered, and the news of Miami's predicament was being broadcast everywhere. Overinflated confidence in the Miami real estate market started to deflate. Publications that formerly glorified "America's Playground" asked why Miami officials could not solve a problem so basic as clearing her channel.

Eventually, the water was pumped from the hold of the *Prinz Valdemar,* enabling her to be heaved upright. Tugs pulled her from the channel and hauled her to the foot of Biscayne Boulevard. Later she was overhauled again and converted into an aquarium.

The building boom, slowed by the *Prinz Valdemar,* suffered a more severe blow by a monster hurricane the following fall. Newspaper headlines around the country seemed that Miami's good fortune was ended. The boom was over for sure, most people said. Others thought it was a good thing, that the *Prinz Valdemar* had performed a valuable service to the area. People would stop the real estate lunacy.

However, the bizarre disaster had amply demonstrated to Miami that harbor improvements were essential if the port was ever to become the major Atlantic port Julia Tuttle had foreseen so many years ago. It was the stimulus that Miami needed. The dredges brought in to open the harbor stayed on to continue widening the channel and the neck of the turning basin. And that was only the beginning. Other improvements, long under consideration, were set in motion.

The frenzied boom times were past. The best was yet to come.

The *Prinz Valdemar,* newly outfitted with lower masts, sporting ·e-catching lights at night and flags during the day, and docked ·ely in concrete, became an institution in Bay Front Park until the ·en she was dismantled to make way for an auditorium. She ·ν ship to survive the devastating hurricane of 1926.

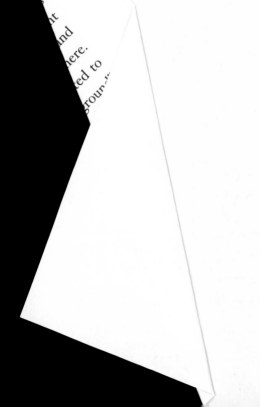

CHAPTER 9

THERE WERE BODIES EVERYWHERE

The Okeechobee Dike Collapse
1928

Storms are a fact of life in Florida. Floridians keep track of them, ignore them if possible, prepare for them if they must, and run from them if there is no other choice. But the one that arrived at Lake Okeechobee on September 16, 1928, was different. First came the watery catastrophe when at least two thousand people died. Then came the aftermath when in the scorching heat, with no water or food and everything familiar gone, the survivors had to search through muck and refuse, gagging at the stench, for the dead bodies of people they knew and perhaps loved.

Some said the actual death count was 3,000, some said 1,836. No one knew for certain. Whatever it was, it was at that time in our country's history one of the worst natural disasters ever, surpassed only by the Galveston hurricane of 1900 when over 8,000 died and the Johnstown flood of 1889, which killed 2,200.

The shore of Lake Okeechobee, the fourth largest natural lake in the United States, was continually changing, depending on the rainfall. Heavy summer rain caused high water in the lake—for it to rise a foot in an hour was not unusual. In the previous decade canals were dug and dikes were built, the dikes being banks of muck from five to nine feet high and twenty to forty feet wide at the base, overgrown with bushes and weeds. They were designed to control the water and drain portions of land for farming. What made risky lake-bottom farming worthwhile was the lush fertility of the black soil. When summer rains caused high water levels, some farmers left the area to reenergize themselves with vacations. In the fall, when things had dried out, they returned to start planting. Most of those who stayed in the area in summer made it through the unproductive months, feeding their families by distilling whiskey. Moonshining, illegal but believed harmless, provided a good livelihood in the remote backwoods of the Everglades where sugar cane, a necessary ingredient, grew profusely.

Due to heavy rains lake levels were already high in September when residents of the southern shore communities began hearing radio reports about a storm doing extensive damage in Puerto Rico. There seemed to be little cause for concern. Some took halfhearted precautions, but mostly people simply remained alert. That changed at 7:45 p.m. when a radio announcer, in the midst of an announcement that stated there was no danger to Florida, excitedly broke off in mid-sentence, saying the storm had hit Palm Beach and it was devastating. At that very moment water was creeping into the towns located at the lower end of Lake Okeechobee, and within minutes lakewater had entered some homes.

The southern end of Lake Okeechobee is shaped like a funnel, with communities formed on the small islands situated there. The islands, Big Kreamer, Little Kreamer, Torry, and Ritta Island, were almost frost-free and considered to be the best farm land in the entire Everglades. They were also first to be affected by the mounting calamity.

Although seemingly protected by the rows of Australian pines that had been planted on Kreamer Island to serve as windbreaks for avocado groves, many of the island's small houses simply lifted off

Trucks loaded with coffins after the disaster.
FLORIDA PHOTOGRAPHIC COLLECTION/FLORIDA STATE ARCHIVES

their foundations, bashed against the pines, and were swept a half mile away.

Ross Winne and his wife, owners of a two-story hotel on Kreamer Island, were among the few who chose to leave for West Palm Beach. Winne thought his neighbors were not using common sense. "The north wind is going to keep piling water up in this bay. There will be no undertow to let it flow back," he said. "There is no reason it couldn't get as high as the dike. . . . No wonder the lake is rising. I am not afraid of wind, and I am not afraid of water, but when you get too much of both at once, it's time to leave!"

By the time Torry Island residents decided to evacuate, the causeway was flooded, forcing twenty-three people to return to the Aunapu Packing House and frantically climb onto tractors and crates for safety. When the building collapsed, they were plunged into the surging black waters, some caught in trees, others clutching at floating debris. Ten of those twenty-three people died.

On the mainland the town of Chosen was at the base of the funnel. With the water level already high, the intense, sustained winds of the storm pushed it even higher, putting maximum stress on the dirt levee. When the levee breached, the water flushed away everything in its path.

In Pat Burke's one-story frame house, built a quarter mile from the dike, Pat and his family, along with his brother and sister and their families, climbed to the attic where the men frantically hacked a hole in the roof, no easy task through the corrugated iron that covered the original boards. All nineteen people managed to wriggle through the hole and were clinging to the roof in the pitch blackness when the dike broke. A huge wave roared through, toppling the house completely so that it came to rest on one side of the roof. Of the nineteen family members, just two survived, hanging on, desperately clinging there until morning.

Twenty Chosen residents who sought shelter in Isaac West's store, watched the store's roof sail away, then packed themselves into a bathroom. A neighbor's house floated by so gently that the two families inside it did not realize they were moving until the house slammed into a railroad embankment.

Belle Glade, the largest town on the lake shore, suffered the greatest loss of life and the most property damage. Many residents sought safety in the town's two hotels, Riedel's and Tedder's. The only building to emerge nearly unscathed was Tedder's Hotel, which had been constructed of sturdy material purchased from the demolition of one wing of Henry Flagler's magnificent Royal Poinciana Hotel in Palm Beach. Walter Greer, the mayor of Belle Glade, a big, robust man, organized confused people who had been milling aimlessly about into pairs, one man to one woman. He ordered them to stick together, no matter what, as they headed for Tedder's Hotel. Somehow, it happened that his two adult daughters had paired off, but their mother realized they were missing and was frantic. When someone said they had been seen in a nearby building that lost its roof, Greer dashed outside to investigate. Knocked to his feet again and again, he doggedly searched under the wreckage until he was certain his girls were not there. He then made his way back to the hotel; his wife by that time was nearly hysterical. On a hunch and trying to calm her, Greer headed out once more, checking this time at Riedel's Hotel where he found the girls safe and not anxious to return to Tedder's through the driving rain and thigh-high water. Greer struggled mightily back to the other hotel again, reported to his wife, fell into a deep sleep, and slept undisturbed until morning.

Those who survived the night could hardly believe what their eyes beheld the next morning. Parts of houses, trees, beds, and wrecked cars jutted from the knee-high water. Whole buildings had disappeared, some moved a half mile away, some sat crazily upside down. Just six buildings were still on their foundations. Streets were packed with refuse as high as a tall man's head. Black mud covered everything, but worst of all, there were bodies everywhere. The sun emerged as the first two bodies, a little girl and her brother, were gently placed on a pool table. It wasn't long, however, before the other tables were full and the floor was full, too.

There was so much work to be done, but there were no tools, nothing to work with. Help was slow in coming since means of communication and transportation were all but nonexistent. Into this chaos stepped a real-life hero, Dr. William Buck, a take-charge man who put his experience as a former army major to good use by first organizing local legionnaires to recruit volunteers, many of whom were still needed by their own families.

Drinking water was of the utmost importance for people doing manual labor in the Florida sun, so the doctor had men bring ice from a storage house to melt for drinking water. He then ordered all women to take the children to Palm Beach—42 miles away. There was no transportation, but about one hundred women made the walk, knowing there was nothing useful they could do in the lake region.

The men, haggard, hungry, thirsty, began searching through the wreckage for bodies. They kept at it for days. The intense heat caused bodies to deteriorate so rapidly it soon was impossible to determine even the race of the dead person. The stench was overwhelming, not only from human remains but from dead fish, alligators, and other animals. At first carpenters made rough coffins with pieces of wood from wrecked houses, but so many were needed that after a while they loaded the bodies into a truck like cordwood, hauled them to a common grave dug by steam shovel, and buried them. Steam shovels dug two mass graves in West Palm Beach, one for white people and one for blacks. Small boats searched the lake, hauling about six bodies at a time back through the water, each fastened to the boat by a rope tied about the neck. Then a crew wearing disinfected gloves hauled the bodies and stacked them in piles. After a time few bodies were buried; instead they were soaked with crude oil and cremated in piles of a dozen or more. Some bodies were eaten in the canals by alligators, some were never found. Over the years farmers found the skeletons of flood victims in their fields.

"Doc" Buck also started the work of clearing highways, an enormous job with many of them under water, some piled high with houses, hyacinths, carcasses, and tall Australian pine trees. Because of the highway situation, few people outside the immediate area understood the seriousness of the Lake Okeechobee catastrophe. Even the governor was unaware of the situation until Wednesday, but he arrived five days after the storm, apologizing to the survivors.

Afterward he said: "In six miles between Pahokee and Belle Glade I counted twenty-seven corpses in the water or on the roadside but not taken from the water. Total dead on the roadside and not buried and counted but not in plank coffins was one hundred and twenty-six. In six additional miles more than five hundred and thirty-seven bodies were already interred. Fifty-seven additional bodies were hauled out of this area today in trucks and tonight four truck loads of bodies

Wooden coffins stacked along the canal, awaiting removal.
FLORIDA PHOTOGRAPHIC COLLECTION/FLORIDA STATE ARCHIVES

were brought from adjoining areas by boat, loaded and sent to West Palm Beach for burial. One military officer reported to me that while in Belle Glade today for thirty minutes, ten bodies were brought in and added to the pile of bodies, thirty-seven in one pile and sixty in the other."

Next day, an editorial in the *Everglades News* portrayed the situation as follows: "Relief workers who have labored in the Glades section for days are worn out. They need to be replaced by others, for they have almost reached the limit of human endurance. In many instances there are inadequate sleeping accommodations for these workers. Additional cots have been requisitioned, with blankets and clothing. Food supplies are available in plenty and in the stricken towns the water supply is said to have been rehabilitated. The great need now is for workers and for means of spreading disinfectants."

Incredibly, another problem for the relief workers was the rude intrusion of curiosity seekers. It became such a dreadful interference that the National Guard had to station troops just to keep out the morbid pests. Even some minor officials from the outside tried to take advantage of their positions to gawk, and in the process they got in the way of overworked relief workers. One U.S. federal marshal from Miami, fortified with alcohol, became so obnoxious, Deputy Sheriff Winne handcuffed him and had him sent back to Miami.

Although alcohol was illegal, it was quietly permitted for the workers in the devastated area. It is doubtful if many people could have proceeded with the dismal work for long without whatever relief alcohol provided. The hard physical labor, the heat, the fatigue, the sleeplessness, the stench and sight of decomposed bodies and body parts, the occasional heartbreak of identifying those bodies or body parts as belonging to someone they loved—it was almost unbearable, and no one, including officers of the law, would deny workers a drink of whiskey if it helped them.

President Herbert Hoover toured the Lake Okeechobee region the following February, and that same year the state legislature approved funds for a new, huge rock levee, specified to be eighteen to twenty feet higher than the lake's level.

CHAPTER 10

A BLACK WALL OF WATER

Veterans' Rescue Train Wiped Out

1935

In 1924, when the U.S. Congress voted to give bonuses to World War I veterans, to be paid in 1945, the country had not yet fallen into the bleak years of the Great Depression. By 1932, however, many veterans were unemployed, homeless, and hungry. They joined together to form the Bonus Expeditionary Force, better known as the Bonus Army, and peacefully invaded Washington, D.C., demanding what was rightfully theirs. As they set up camps in the capital, they maintained tight military order while awaiting a vote from Congress. Although the House passed a bill to award their payments, the Senate did not, and the "Death March" that the veterans started in front of the Capitol lasted a month until President Herbert Hoover ordered the removal of the men from government property. Under the leadership of General Douglas MacArthur, and with assistance from Major Dwight Eisenhower and Major George Patton, troops advanced with fixed bayonets, machine guns, and tanks, tossing tear gas to rout the bewildered veterans from their camps. They were stunned to receive such treatment from their government.

Along with the deteriorating economic picture, his sending troops against former war heroes sealed Hoover's fate in the next election. He lost resoundingly to Franklin D. Roosevelt.

Putting men to work was at the heart of Roosevelt's program, and one of the ways he meant to achieve that goal was by founding the Civilian Conservation Corps, a military-style organization of young men who worked for a dollar a day, plus food and clothing, and who would plant trees, build bridges, and fight forest fires. So it was that a group of 25,000 ill-fed, inadequately clothed, demoralized young men were brought to Florida to begin construction of a highway intended to run parallel to Henry Flagler's fabled East Coast Railway Extension along Florida's east coast all the way to Key West.

When construction on the Florida East Coast Railway Key West Extension was begun in 1905, it was the second largest construction project in the world, second only to the Panama Canal. Flagler, former Standard Oil partner of John D. Rockefeller, had built luxury hotels along Florida's east coast and constructed the East Coast Railway system to link them. Flagler's project to extend the rail line from Miami to Key West at times employed more than 4,000 men. It was an undertaking variously called impractical, unthinkable, impossible, and "Flagler's Folly." Frank Stoneman, editor of Miami's daily newspaper, whose daughter Marjorie Stoneman Douglas would become famous as an author and champion of the Everglades, warned that the solid rock embankments being built were the wrong structures to build and that bridges instead of solid fills should be built, but he was ignored. What did a newsman know about building railroads? From 1912 when it was completed until 1935, the Key West Extension had successfully carried an estimated fifty million passengers on the 156-mile journey across a string of islands to America's most southern city.

However, the Depression hit the Keys with the same devastation as it did the rest of the nation, fomenting all sorts of plans to galvanize the economy, including ways to encourage more tourism. Some thought a modern highway for automotive traffic would be a power-ful stimulant to the economy, and with the election of Roosevelt, the signs that one would be built were encouraging. Funds from the Public Works Administration became available and the newly estab-lished Civilian Conservation Corps would provide the labor. Hopes soared as the project was begun.

Until everything could be assembled for the highway construc-tion, the first group of men who arrived at the Keys in 1934 were put to work building living quarters for themselves. More men soon arrived, bringing the total to 684 housed at three camps, one on Windley Key and one at each end of Lower Metacumbe Key. Each man was paid $30 a month, of which $25 was sent to his wife or family. The family's small sum enabled them to buy a few necessities, which in turn helped stimulate the national economy. The man's work helped preserve our natural resources and build some lasting structures for the country.

Since everything needed for the project had to be supplied by barges, which did not always arrive when expected, shortages of food, water, clothing, and medical provisions were common. Working and living conditions for the men were not the best, but their previous existence had not been easy either.

Most of the veterans camped in the Keys were from out of state, northerners mostly, and not knowledgeable about tropical weather. On Saturday, August 31, when the Jacksonville Weather Bureau announced a "tropical disturbance" in the Bahamas, even native Floridians were not unduly alarmed.

Ernest Hemingway, at his home on Whitehead Street in Key West, was working on a new novel when he heard the weather report. He was not much concerned but nevertheless occasionally checked later reports until he decided it would be a good idea to add extra lines to his treasured boat, *Pilar,* and hope for the best.

On Sunday the Keys were advised that the storm was moving due west at 8 miles per hour, and people definitely began paying attention, though not making serious preparations. There was an understanding that in an emergency, the Florida East Coast Railway office would evacuate the veterans by chartered train, but the announcement at 1:30 p.m. on Labor Day stated the Keys should expect only gales, not an emergency. However, by 4:41 p.m., advisories indicated the storm was heading for the Keys, which aroused concern among authorities at the veterans' camp. On Monday morning, Labor Day, Ray Sheldon, who was in charge while his chief was away, called the Florida East Coast office in Miami to determine how long it would take for them to have a train come to evacuate the workers. Told it would take three hours, he then contacted his boss, who gave the order to start the evacuation to Hollywood, 18 miles north of Miami.

The order went out immediately, but calling in a railroad crew on Labor Day proved to be a challenge, besides which no engine was available until 3:00 p.m., and then it took two hours to steam up the locomotive. The engineer, J. J. Haycraft, was called at 3:10 p.m., and he immediately assembled his train of six coaches, two baggage cars, and three boxcars, only to discover one car required some repairs that delayed leaving until 4:25. His frustration must have soared when he was held back yet again for another ten minutes at the Miami River drawbridge to accommodate heavy holiday boat traffic.

Finally, as the skies continued to darken ominously, Haycraft sped his train south to Homestead where he, his conductor, and his trainmaster conferred and concluded it would be better to reverse the train engine, back the train all the way south, so that the engine with its bright headlight would face forward on the trip back. They were certain the return trip would be an ordeal of navigating into blackness. That maneuver took until 5:15, but it was followed by another glitch when a derrick beside the track snared the engine and had to be unhooked, eating up another hour and twenty minutes.

The storm was hitting full force by the time the train reached Windley Key, where Haycraft could see a group of people huddled

Remains of the FEC rescue train, with only the engine upright after
the storm surge. HISTORICAL MUSEUM OF SOUTHERN FLORIDA

together near the track, hoping for something—*anything*—to help
them. He was after all employed by the railroad, charged with rescuing men for the railroad, but, giving no thought to whether or not he
ought to do it, Haycraft stopped the engine, waited for the people to
scramble aboard, started up the engine again, and found to his horror
that the train would not move. His crew discovered that a freakishly
torn cable held them at a standstill and had to be cut before they
could start up again. Another delay—when every second counted.
Buffeted by 200 mile per hour winds, blinded to the point that
Haycraft ran right past the station, the train ended up a few miles farther at Islamadora, where Haycraft waited while the terrified, screaming people ran to the train. By that time huge waves were crashing
over tracks that had been built 7 feet above sea level.

Haycraft's engine, number 447, weighed 320,000 pounds, but
when the waves took a boxcar right off the tracks behind him, the

engine lurched violently, automatically locking the air brakes on the whole train. At that point Haycraft, his conductor, and his fireman were all in the cab, watching helplessly as a 20-foot-high black wall that was a tidal wave blasted all the cars from the track as if they were toy trains. The people he had just rescued were trapped as waves poured into the cars through pulverized windows. More than 577 veterans and civilians were gone in an instant.

When rescue parties arrived by barge on Tuesday night, the island was cleared, swept clean by waves, the camps gone as though they never existed. Dead bodies lay everywhere, even hanging from the few trees that remained. Miles of railroad track stretched over the ground, twisted like pretzels. Counted among the few fortunate survivors were the dozen workers who had gone without permission to Key West for the weekend, jobless again but undoubtedly counting their blessings.

The Coast Guard sent up seaplanes on searching expeditions, but it was volunteers from the American Legion who did the grim, up-close combing through wreckage and caring for those they found. Doctors and nurses worked around the clock in a church in Homestead, treating the few people who were alive. Fingerprint experts arrived from Washington with orders from President Roosevelt that each body be identified and have a separate coffin as a sign of respect. The president was unaware as were the experts who soon learned that the hot Florida sun decomposed bodies so rapidly that proper identification was not possible after a few days. Other experts warned of the possibility of epidemics if burials were not performed quickly. Accordingly, unidentified bodies were piled into a funeral pyre and cremated while a Protestant minister, a Jewish rabbi, and a Catholic priest took turns saying prayers.

Ernest Hemingway joined a rescue party as soon as he was able to reach the area. He was appalled to see so many bodies, was quoted as saying, "You could find them face down and face up in the mangroves.

Body of victim being loaded onto a rescue boat at Snake Creek.
HISTORICAL MUSEUM OF SOUTHERN FLORIDA

Then further on you found them high in the trees where the water had swept them, beginning to be too big for their blue jeans and jackets that they could never fill when they were on the bum and hungry."

When at last the outside world learned of the extent of the disaster, there was outrage as to why the Weather Bureau had not alerted people sooner and why the government hadn't acted sooner to save the veterans. The widespread fury led to a Congressional investigation.

Few people attracted more attention than an enraged Ernest Hemingway. "Who sent nearly a thousand war veterans, many of them husky, hard-working and simply out of luck, but many of them close to the border of pathological cases, to live in frame shacks on the Florida Keys in hurricane months?" he blasted in the cover article of the journal *New Masses*. "Who advised against sending the train from Miami to evacuate the veterans until four-thirty o'clock on Monday so that it was blown off the tracks before it ever reached the lower camps?"

Hemingway soon had his answers. A Congressional investigation pronounced the catastrophe an act of God, absolving all the aforementioned parties of blame.

The fears of newspaper man Frank Stoneman were partially realized, but although some of the solid embankments built for the East Coast Railroad had washed away, many of Flagler's structures were still intact. There were those who said "Flagler's Folly" should be repaired, the railway extension rebuilt. That it was possible was proved by the East Coast Railroad when it replaced damaged track within the month in order to run the costly engine back to Miami. All of the bridges and much of the roadbed still stood, the roadbeds repairable.

The nation, however, was caught in the great Depression and the Flagler railroad was bankrupt. To rescue the railway was not anyone's priority, especially with the bourgeoning popularity of the automobile. The government granted the East Coast Railroad permission to close the rail line, enabling it to sell all its structures for the construction of the Overseas Highway.

A monument was built on Islamorada to honor those whose lives were lost in the calamity. President Roosevelt sent a telegram that was read at the dedication. It said, "I join in the dedication of the monument to those who met death in the awful visitation that swept the Florida Keys on Labor Day, 1935. The disaster which made desolate the heart of so many of our people brought a personal sorrow to me because some years ago, I knew many residents of the Keys. I tender to all whose hearts were torn by the loss of loved ones an assurance of heart-felt sympathy."

CHAPTER 11

A SURPRISE ATTACK

Gulfamerica's Maiden Voyage
1942

It was April 10, just four months after the carnage at Pearl Harbor, but Pearl Harbor was far away and did not yet seem real to many Americans. It surely was the furthest thing from the minds of the two teenage couples who were on a double date, riding the merry-go-round at Jacksonville Beach that evening. Friday night, after all, was date night and bars and restaurants were crowded. The only thing out of the ordinary was there seemed to be more sailors than usual from the nearby Jacksonville Naval Air Station whooping it up on weekend passes. Otherwise, the usual good-humored crowd milled about the streets and along the beaches, having a fun time. As it turned out, it would be a night even the teenagers would remember vividly sixty years later.

Seagoing freighters could often be seen from the eastern shore. The frequency of the traffic in the shipping lanes off the entire East Coast increased as the United States stepped up efforts to keep her old ally, Great Britain, provided with fuel oil, aluminum, and whatever else she needed to hold Germany at bay. In retaliation German U-boats escalated their attacks on the civilian ships carrying supplies until, in the month of March, there was an average of one sinking per day, which led the U.S. Navy to describe the region as "the most dangerous area for merchant shipping in the entire world."

The petroleum industry was up in arms about the loss of their tankers on the Maine-to-Florida and the Caribbean runs. The loss of lives and the financial damages were bad enough, but the resulting lowering of morale among workers due to ship sinkings was also caus-ing a drain on men signing up for work. A concerned committee of oil industry executives held a meeting and came up with some recom-mendations they hoped to see adopted, among them, installing swing-ing guns on all tankers and manning them with U.S. Navy guards. They also suggested that lights on shore facing the ocean be "suppressed" to avoid silhouetting ships as targets for the Germans.

A nightly blackout of shore lights was strongly resisted by Florida businesspeople who had any connection to tourism, the state's larg-est industry. Beach resort operators and restaurant and bar owners all objected to anything that interfered with their businesses. As a consequence the commander of the Atlantic Fleet acceded, asking for only a dimout, so that the brightest lights would not highlight passing tankers. It would prove to be a disastrous error on his part.

On the same day the Atlantic Fleet commander was vetoing the blackout, a freighter was sunk off the shore of Atlantic City, New Jersey, with the loss of twenty crewmen. One crewman said that as he looked back at the shore from his lifeboat the "lights were like Coney Island." Another complained: "We might as well run with our lights on."

One of the first tankers to be fitted out with guns was the 8,000-ton SS *Gulfamerica,* the Gulf Oil Corporation's brand new ship, which was making her maiden voyage that April evening. The *Gulfamerica,* with 90,000 barrels of fuel oil, had a crew of forty-one, plus the seven Navy armed guards who were to handle her guns on the run north to New York City. Oscar Anderson, her master, ran the *Gulfamerica* at a good speed, with her lights out, her radios silent. Two guards stood facing forward as lookouts on top of the pilot house and two more were on guard at the rear of the ship.

On the previous April evening, the commander of a German U-boat, the U-123, twenty-eight-year-old Lieutenant Commander Reinhard Hardegen, had managed to avoid detection as he surveyed the north Florida coastal area around the mouth of the St. Johns River. From what he could observe, he was becoming convinced the Mayport Naval Center was not the important military threat he had been led to believe it was. After spending the day 3 miles offshore underwater, he brought the U-boat back to the shipping lane that evening, sighted the *Gulfamerica,* and chased her for over an hour until closing in on her off Jacksonville Beach. At 10:20 p.m., with one of his two remaining torpedoes, Hardegen scored a direct hit on the shiny new tanker, severing her in two and lighting up the sky.

Captain Anderson ordered his engines stopped, lifeboats lowered, and his civilian crew was told to abandon ship. While *Gulfamerica*'s radio operator was sending last-minute calls for assistance, Captain Anderson crammed important confidential papers into a weighted pouch and tossed it overboard. Possibly due to the total surprise of the attack, the Navy guards had not had time to fire a single shot from their new guns.

A teenage couple riding the merry-go-round had just come around and were facing directly toward the ocean when the torpedoes hit the ship, exploding in a giant fireball. The sight was spectacular, but like many others who lived on the coast, the teenagers were totally ignorant as to what was going on in the shipping lanes just offshore. They thought what they saw must have been the result of a collision of two tankers. Thousands of other people interrupted their Friday night celebrations in the nightclubs, drive-ins, restaurants, and other beachside amusement plazas. They surged on to the beach, watching with growing horror as the flames leaped ever higher and the sickening smell of the black smoky clouds drifted in from the sea.

German Commander Hardegen saw that he was successful in slicing the *Gulfamerica* in two but to be sure both sections would sink, he readied his deck guns to shell the damaged tanker. As his men prepared to carry out the order, the commander noted that there were thousands of innocent civilians gathered directly in line behind the wounded tanker, and he also observed for the first time how many homes were built close to the beach. Hardegen did not know whether or not there were any guns aimed in the direction of the ocean, but he thought it worth the risk of being hit by gunfire and possibly going aground in order not to shell any civilians. He repositioned his U-boat in the shallower water between the shore and the damaged tanker, shelling outward toward the ocean until he was satisfied the tanker was no longer operational. He then began hastily but carefully withdrawing from the area.

When the shelling began, twenty-five *Gulfamerica* crewmen attempted to escape by jumping overboard, but most all of them were lost, as was a lifeboat that capsized. *Gulfamerica*'s chief engineer and two others from the ship tried to rescue more of the crew from their lifeboat, but the flames and heat from the burning fuel prevented them from continuing. These men later reported, with surprise and gratitude, that the Germans made no attempt to shell the crew members in lifeboats, their aim most likely being to prevent the fuel from being shipped, not to kill helpless civilians.

Horrified spectators on shore wasted no time spreading the news, anxiously telephoning friends and relatives. Before long, the area was inundated with sightseers, most of whom were turned away by the military. Rescue boats arrived quickly from Mayport to pick up any injured survivors and retrieve dead bodies from the water.

Although most of the onshore observers were shocked into near paralysis, there were a few heroes or would-be heroes. One who would fall into the latter category was a tourist who, full of good intentions and sincerely wanting to help in the rescue, set off for the wreck in a small rowboat. By the time he reached the scene of the tragedy, the wind had picked up considerably and he was unable to maneuver against its force. The good-intentioned man was picked up the next day, 20 miles offshore.

Townsend Hawkes, a year-round citizen, was the first to notify Jacksonville Naval Base as to what was happening. He then telephoned city authorities, alerting them to black out the beach lights to prevent the town from being shelled. After running nearly a mile to a dock where he and another man launched a small boat, they rowed out to the tanker, intending to pick up survivors. The strong wind interfered with their plans, pushing them dangerously close to the burning oil slick. Eventually even the would-be rescuers were picked up by a cutter from the Mayport Naval Base. Hawkes would later serve a four-year stint in the Coast Guard, much of it combatting German U-boats.

As Commander Hardegen was fleeing from the scene, planes from the Jacksonville Air Station sped to the area, dropping flares to mark his position, which was then shelled by a U.S. destroyer that had arrived at the location. Although the destroyer inflicted severe damage on the U-boat, the German commander managed to work his way out of the channel, into the ocean, and crawl to his home port on the coast of France, which was occupied by Germany at that time.

The following day, April 11, local government authorities posted rules about nighttime lights amid caustic remarks about locking the barn after the horses were stolen. Just the same, there were to be no bright lights or any neon signs lit along the shore. Cars were forbidden on the beach after dark and all cars traveling east of the Intracoastal Waterway were directed to use nothing brighter than parking lights at night. Homes along the beachfront were ordered to use blackout curtains.

On April 16, 1942, the first and final voyage of the *Gulfamerica* ended when what remained of her sank to the ocean floor. The tanker would fulfill one more mission as an artificial reef.

More than 250,000 merchant mariners volunteered to do the hazardous work of delivering supplies, tanks, troops, or whatever was needed to win the war. Nearly 9,000 died during World War II, at a rate of one in twenty-four. Indeed, the merchant marine had the largest ratio of casualties of any of the branches of the service. General Douglas MacArthur once said, "I hold no branch in higher esteem than the merchant marine service." The *New York Times* in 1944 would praise "these intrepid civilians," saying, "D-Day would not have been possible without them."

It was ironic, then, and tragic, that the survivors of the wreck of the *Gulfamerica* and other merchant marine shipwrecks, wounded and some barely surviving, were dismayed when they learned they were not eligible for any medical benefits or compensation of any kind. They did receive a certificate of thanks, but that wouldn't pay the bills.

Wartime president Franklin D. Roosevelt had predicted, "As time goes on, there will be greater public understanding of our merchant fleet's record during this war." It didn't seem to happen. One patriotic man who had joined the merchant marine because the other branches of service rejected him due to minor medical reasons was determined to serve his country. He served on a merchant ship that was torpedoed and sunk, spent thirty-one days adrift on a lifeboat, and when it was all over, he was told he wasn't a veteran.

Further adding to the ignominy, most of the merchant ships sunk in World War II had no federal protection and were fair game in peacetime for deep-water divers who raided the wrecks and carried off ship bells, other brass fixtures, and in one case where dynamite was used, a propeller. Wrecks of government ships were protected by federal law and anyone removing anything from their sites could be jailed, but it was open season on civilian ships.

Survivors of the merchant marine wrecks and families were incensed, claiming the ships were cemeteries, hallowed ground. The daughter of A. M. Johanson, the master of a Standard Oil Company tanker who died when his ship was torpedoed and shelled in 1942, agreed. Speaking of her father's wrecked ship, she said, "That is his grave. It seems there's nothing sacred anymore."

One survivor of the *Gulfamerica* hired a diver to search his cabin and try to retrieve his dog tags and wallet. He was dismayed to learn the ship had been dynamited on the ocean floor by divers to haul away the propeller for the brass. "You wouldn't treat the *Arizona* that way," he said sadly.

Finally, in 1988, so many years after the war ended, the United States government recognized members of the merchant marine as veterans. A few years later, the surviving members received discharge papers. Their proud response? "We Delivered the Goods."

CHAPTER 12

A GREAT AVIATION MYSTERY

The Disappearance of Flight 19
1945

The legend began at 2:10 on the clear afternoon of December 5, 1945, when five Avenger torpedo bombers, designated Flight 19 under the command of Lieutenant Charles Taylor, left Fort Lauderdale Naval Air Station on a routine training mission and were never seen again. Each plane carried a crew of three, but one man was absent that day. When a giant Martin Mariner, with a crew of thirteen, was sent to search for the missing planes, it also disappeared, launching a great aviation mystery.

The Avengers were scheduled to fly east for 160 miles, then north for 40 miles, and back to the base in a routine flight for the crews who were nearing the end of their training. Estimated time for the flight was about two hours, but in an hour and a half, Taylor, an experienced Pacific flight veteran, became convinced his compasses were not working and that he was lost. Conventional wisdom for pilots in the area was, if lost, immediately switch the radio to the emergency frequency for better communication and head west, but Taylor had only recently been stationed in the Fort Lauderdale area, having spent much time at the Miami Air Station, where the admonition to head west could land a plane in the Gulf of Mexico. Taylor continued the flight on dead reckoning, believing the islands he saw below him were the Florida Keys, not the islands of the Bahamas as was later believed. Because radio contact was spotty, Fort Lauderdale advised him to change to the emergency frequency to improve communication, but he refused, fearing he might lose contact with his planes during the changeover. At approximately 5:00 p.m. the base heard two of Taylor's students over the air waves. One said, "If we would just fly west, we would get home." Another repeated that later.

A bad situation turned worse when severe weather moved in with sunset at 5:29. It was estimated the planes had enough fuel to last until 8:00 p.m. Bases from Melbourne to Key West were ordered to turn on their field lights and beacons.

At 6:00 the Sea Frontier Evaluation Center in Miami, using direction bearings from other coastal centers, calculated the approximate position for Flight 19—east of New Smryna Beach, farther north than anyone had guessed. Search planes from Vero Beach, Daytona, and Miami were dispatched into the stormy, dark skies.

At the Banana River Naval Air Station, two Martin Mariner PBM seaplanes, Training 32 and Training 49, were dispatched to fly to the position fix supplied by Miami to join the search. At 8:30, T32 reported arriving at the area but T49 did not.

Mariners were sometimes called "flying gas tanks" because of the gas fumes that could frequently be smelled inside them. An explosion could be ignited by a single spark. Although this one was later said to have vanished without a trace, it was probably the explosion in the sky observed by a ship at 7:50 p.m. The timing and location would indicate T49 was in the right location, but no further communication was received from the plane.

In 1945 there was no Global Positioning System (GPS) to guide pilots flying over water. To calculate their position pilots had to know their starting point, time, speed, and the direction they had flown.

Without landmarks, flying over the ocean could be tricky. Although Taylor was an experienced pilot with over 2,500 hours flying time, including over 600 of them in Avengers, he hadn't flown much in the Bahamas and apparently became confused, convinced his compasses were not working. He had his planes turn several more times, and with visibility worsening so too did his confusion.

By the morning of December 6, more than 200 planes from Jacksonville, Vero Beach, Boca Raton, Orlando, Sarasota, Tampa, Miami, and Daytona had joined a search for the Avengers that covered more than 400 miles, accompanied by sixteen ships patrolling the waters. Rough seas caused difficulties for the ships, which had also answered calls from several other ships in trouble, including one carrying troops home from the European theater of war.

Workloads increased dramatically over the next few days, with false sightings that had to be checked out, reports of oil slicks, mysterious lights, pools of blood and debris, none of which were significant. No wreckage from Flight 19 was ever found. Avengers, nicknamed "Iron Birds," weighed 14,000 pounds empty. One pilot said, "When they ditched, they went down pretty fast." Then too, if they had flown as far east as the continental shelf, a definite possibility, the ocean there drops to several thousand feet, quickly swallowing wreckage from planes or ships.

On April 3, 1946, an official Navy statement was issued. "It is believed that the flight leader's false assurance of identifying as the Florida Keys, islands he sighted, plagued his future decisions and confused his reasoning. . . . At 6:00 he was directing his flight to fly east . . . even though he was undoubtedly east of Florida." The Naval Board of Inquiry issued a list of fifty-six facts, with fifty-six opinions based on those facts. Opinion 44 said that "this disappearance . . . was caused by a temporary mental confusion resulting in faulty judgment on the part of the instructor, Lt. Charles Taylor, in permitting himself to lose knowledge of his general position relative to the peninsula of Florida, and failure on his part to utilize the facilities available to him for orienting himself." Opinion 45 continued: "No serious blame incurred by any known person other than that which may be assigned to Lt. Charles Taylor for his faulty judgment that contributed to his disappearance."

Rumors abounded, many concerning Lieutenant Taylor. He had tried to be excused from the flight the day prior to it, not an unusual occurrence according to many of the men. However, there was no one to take his place. A rumor persisted that he was hungover. Some friends said he seldom drank, while others said he did. According to some, he had already ditched planes over water due to his own errors in past flights, but others said they would trust their lives to him without question.

Not everyone agreed with the fifty-six facts and opinions, most notably Lieutenant Taylor's widowed mother and an aunt who had helped raise him. Their constant badgering and letter-writing campaign eventually led to another hearing by the Correction Board, concluding with an announcement on November 19, 1947, in which an assistant secretary for the navy advised Mrs. Taylor that "after a careful and conscientious consideration of all the factors of the case," the board considered that the flight had disappeared for "causes or reasons unknown." The finger of blame no longer pointed solely at Lieutenant Taylor.

Although Taylor's mother and aunt were not entirely satisfied, the incident gradually faded from public consciousness until a writer, Allan Eckert, recalled the episode in an article for the *American Legion Magazine* in the April 1962 issue. Eckert resurrected some of the old quotes, added some of his own exaggerated ones, and caused a bit of a stir. Then, in 1964 Vincent Gaddis, writing for February's *Argosy* magazine, contributed to the theatrics with more unsubstantiated quotes and talk of strange occurrences and possible atmospheric aberrations, adding that at the time the planes disappeared, the weather

A PBM Mariner aircraft. Two disappeared during the search for the Avengers.
NATIONAL MUSEUM OF AVIATION

had been perfect and the pilots experts, neither of which was accurate. It was Gaddis who introduced the phrase "Bermuda Triangle" into the American lexicon to label the area roughly bound by Bermuda, Puerto Rico, and Fort Lauderdale. But it was Charles Berlitz, of Fort Lauderdale, a member of the famous language school family, who made the Bermuda Triangle well known to most of the country and the world. His book, *The Bermuda Triangle,* published in 1974, sold over five million hardbound copies and even more in paperback. Berlitz, a great fan of the psychic Edgar Cayce, wrote other books about mysterious phenomena such as the lost continent of Atlantis and, later, the UFOs in Roswell, New Mexico. He was criticized by reviewers as having sensationalized facts, but his Triangle book was nevertheless an overnight best seller. Thus the legend of the Bermuda Triangle was catapulted into the public consciousness. Theories concerning time warps, alien abductions to Mars, and magnetic aberrations circulated nationwide.

In 1975 Lawrence D. Kusche, a librarian at Arizona State University, who also was an experienced pilot, was receiving so many questions about the Bermuda Triangle that he couldn't find answers for, he decided to look into it for himself. After an intensive investigation, he published his own book, *The Bermuda Triangle Mystery—Solved,* in which he debunked most of the "facts" written by authors who repeated the pronouncements of other authors without first checking their authenticity.

Some writers claimed that, starting as far back as 1492, even the journals of Columbus, in which he reported having difficulties with his compass and strange lights in the sky, provided early evidence of the existence of the Bermuda Triangle. Kusche reminded readers that magnetic variation was unknown at the time and that the strange lights Columbus saw were most likely meteors.

Another unsolved mystery was that of the *Mary Celeste,* a 103-foot brigantine found abandoned, fully stocked, and in good condition, an intriguing addition to Bermuda Triangle folklore. However, those who included it in the legend of the Triangle failed to mention that the *Mary Celeste* was found between the Azores and Portugal. It was not unusual for those who spread the fable to leave out the location of a happening if it were inconvenient.

A 1909 disappearance was truly unexplained. The world's most famous sailor, Joshua Slocum, who was the first man to sail around the world alone, started on another sea voyage trip from Martha's Vineyard to South America in *Spray,* the famous boat that he had rebuilt himself. He disappeared on the trip, but he and his boat were both aging, and although no one knows what happened to him, it does not necessarily follow that it was an otherworldly experience.

In 1948 a famous jockey, Al Snider, and two friends rented a cabin cruiser and anchored off Sandy Key, at the southern tip of Florida. They rowed a short way in a dinghy to fish but never returned. Although much was made of their disappearance in the Bermuda

Triangle, it was seldom mentioned that there were gale winds of 50 miles per hour that evening, enough to easily swamp a dinghy with three men crowded into it.

When a British troop transport plane with thirty-nine people aboard was lost on a trip to Jamaica in 1953, the Bermuda Triangle again led news dispatches, omitting the fact that the ship was lost 900 miles to the north.

Harry Conover, a millionaire publisher and outstanding sailor, was the owner of the "best sailboat in ocean racing." In 1958 he and a crew of four friends vanished on a trip from Key West to Miami. Fans of the Triangle myth believed reports that seas were calm, but in truth there were near-hurricane winds, more than enough to capsize the sailboat.

The submarine *Scorpion* was lost at sea in 1968, a reported victim of the Bermuda Triangle. In truth the sub was much closer to Africa and Portugal than it was to the east coast of the United States.

And so it went. The university librarian methodically debunked most of the mysterious disasters of the sea propagated by the linguist. Some experts noted that most of the associated disasters could be explained rationally. Other disasters occurred far from the area denoted as the Bermuda Triangle. Besides, as one sage added, "Accidents do happen."

The Naval Historical Center and the U.S. Coast Guard Headquarters stated that they do not recognize the Bermuda Triangle as an official name, finding that the most practical explanations in most instances are environmental and human error. They noted that the so-called Bermuda Triangle is one of the two places on earth where the magnetic compass points toward true north. Compasses normally point to magnetic north. The Devil's Sea near Japan is the other such spot. If the magnetic variation is not compensated for, particularly in steering east or west, a navigator can be in trouble. The navy also stated that the Gulf Stream is extremely swift, turbulent, and quick to wash away any debris from wrecks. The weather there can be unpredictable with sudden storms, and there are extensive shoals, strong currents, and deep trenches. Then too, there are many pleasure boats in the area, often with inexperienced boaters lacking in knowledge of good seamanship.

Recently, a U.S. geochemist theorized that some mysterious disappearances could result from the formation of methane hydrate, a form of methane, in enormous quantities under pressure and in extreme cold (a theory first advanced by the Soviets in the 1920s). Under certain conditions, as on the deep-sea floor, methane hydrate can form naturally. If a ship passed over it, the seas would boil instantly and the ship would plummet to the bottom, gone without a trace. If proven, the theory might erase the last of the remaining mysteries.

In 1946 the Naval Air Station was closed to make way for the new Fort Lauderdale-Hollywood International Airport. Most of the buildings that housed the Naval Air Station have been destroyed, but a small park has been set aside as a memorial to U.S. Naval Flight 19. Every year on December 5, the Naval Air Station Fort Lauderdale Historical Society holds a memorial service to honor the lost men.

CHAPTER 13

A MISSION GONE WRONG

Fire in *Apollo*
1967

On May 25, 1961, President John F. Kennedy challenged U.S. space officials to the greatest test they had ever confronted.

> I believe that this nation should commit itself to achieving the goal, before this decade is out, of landing a man on the moon and returning him safely to earth. No single space project in this period will be more exciting, or more impressive to mankind, or more important for the long-range exploration of space; and none will be so difficult or expensive to accomplish.

Since 1957, when the Soviets launched Sputnik, the world's first orbiting satellite, a visible and inescapable reminder of America's second place in space, the nation lived with feelings of being second-rate and vulnerable. Americans, accustomed to leading the world in technology, were deeply troubled about the upheaval in the balance of power. According to the respected scientist Edward Teller, "Sputnik represented a technological Pearl Harbor." It didn't help that two weeks later, the Soviets orbited a six-ton satellite with a dog aboard while the United States was working on a grapefruit-size satellite that blew up on the launch pad. The Russians scored again in a big way by putting a man into orbit a few weeks before the United States launched its first man in space, Alan Shepard.

Kennedy's science adviser told him he had three choices, to quit, to stay in second place, or to do something dramatic. Three weeks later, before a joint session of Congress, Kennedy issued his challenge.

The National Aeronautics and Space Administration (NASA), established by President Eisenhower, came up with a blueprint for meeting Kennedy's challenge. Project Mercury would put a man in space, Project Gemini would devise docking strategies, and Project Apollo would land a man on the moon and return him. It was exciting, it was exhilarating, and almost no one connected with the space program thought they could do it in the time frame Kennedy had outlined. NASA pulled out all the stops—there was no time to waste. Not only did they have to figure out how to get to the moon, they had to invent the apparatus needed to do it, and manufacture most of that, too.

The nearly deserted strip of Florida's east coast formerly known as the Mosquito Coast swiftly morphed into the Space Coast, with help from an Air Force C-47 that routinely sprayed the area for mosquitoes, much to the delight of the few citizens who lived nearby.

The Vehicle Assembly Building, the largest enclosed space in the world, was constructed to house the space vehicles. It was so big that photographers shot hundreds of rolls of film but were still unable to capture its enormity.

After Shepard's successful flight, Gus Grissom made a second suborbital flight in July 1961, doubling the time spent in space. It was a successful flight until splashdown when the hatch on the module accidentally gave way, allowing water to enter. Grissom, in his bulky space suit, surfaced and swam away from the sinking capsule, treading water until he was rescued by a helicopter.

The next space mission to capture the public's attention was the one in 1962 during which John Glenn became the first American to orbit the earth. It was not a flawless mission, but the ending was what counted. Glenn instantly became the hero everyone was yearning for, as evidenced by the ticker-tape parades, his speech to Congress, and a nationwide outpouring of adulation.

NASA, however, had no time to rest on its laurels; there was always more work to do. President Kennedy's call to prove to the world that the United States was not second best had to be met. Continuing pressure to meet that challenge intensified when events led the Soviets and the United States to face off in the 1962 Cuban missile crisis. However, after that issue was resolved, interest in space exploration cooled until in the mid-1960s. Public opinion polls and some members of Congress suggested that less money should be spent on the space program. NASA lost its most visible booster when Kennedy was assassinated, but fortunately his successor, Lyndon Johnson, was also a fan of the space program, possibly because of his Texas connections to the Houston Mission Control Center.

In 1965 Grissom was chosen to pilot the first manned Gemini mission, a three-orbit flight, with a copilot, John Young. Having had to tread water as he watched the *Liberty Bell 7* sink in 1961 (it was later retrieved), this time Grissom named his Gemini module the *Molly Brown,* after the unsinkable Broadway musical heroine. "This time, nothing is going to sink out from under us," he said. It was an almost flawless flight. One minor molehill was later made into a mountain by a few irate congressmen and doctors when word got out that Grissom and Young had consumed, along with their unappetizing freeze-dried morsels, a corned beef sandwich that had been slipped into the capsule before launch by astronaut Wally Schirra.

By the summer of 1966, a crew was chosen for the first Apollo manned mission. They were to be Gus Grissom, Ed White, the first man to walk in space, and Roger Chaffee, the youngest astronaut,

Astronauts Gus Grissom, Ed White, and Roger Chaffee.
PHOTO COURTESY OF NASA

aged thirty-one. The spacecraft, manufactured by North American
Aviation, was much larger than previous models, weighing in at
twenty-six metric tons when fully fueled, and it was more sophisti-
cated in design. The hatch opened outward, requiring at least ninety
seconds to open under ordinary circumstances.

There had been much criticism of North American Aviation,
which built the *Apollo* spacecraft, but it did make thirty-nine of the
forty-five design changes requested by astronauts. The remaining ones
were less important, and the module was considered ready. When
the astronauts were invited to a meeting to discuss the spacecraft,
they displayed a signed photo of themselves praying before a model
of their *Apollo* capsule. They had been told to practice their backup
procedures religiously, they said, "So here we are practicing."

In a more serious vein, it was noted that fire in the module could be a problem. The command module would be sealed tight, with oxygen inside pressurized to 16.7 psi (pounds per square inch). The astronauts used Velcro to fasten gear in nylon net pouches to places where they could reach them easily. Both the net and the Velcro were known to be flammable. North American Aviation was told to check and be sure nothing that could spark was closer to those items than 4 inches.

The manager of the Missile and Space Division of General Electric made known his unease concerning fire in a letter to the Apollo Spacecraft Program Office (ASPO). "The first fire in a spacecraft may well be fatal," he wrote. His concerns were acknowledged by the ASPO, which added, "Suitable extinguishing agents are not yet developed."

Dr. Emmanuel Roth of the Lovelace Foundation for Medical Education and Research warned that most synthetic materials would incinerate instantly in pure oxygen if ignited. And Dr. Frank Hendel of the Apollo Space Sciences Systems warned that "no fire-fighting methods have yet been developed that can cope with a fire in pure oxygen."

Another problem was with communications. Voice checks were unsatisfactory. Grissom irritably grumbled, "How do you expect to communicate with us in orbit if you can't even talk to us on the pad?" The jumble of wires running over the floor and walls was suspected of causing the static, but it was an on-and-off thing.

Launch day countdowns were rehearsed several times before an actual launch. On January 27, 1967, there was no fuel in the Saturn rocket, but everything else duplicated countdown procedures as closely as possible, while the spacecraft remained on Pad 34. The simulation moved along nicely; even the voice checks were clear.

Grissom, White, and Chaffee, in their spacesuits, entered the *Apollo* at 1:00 p.m. Grissom's first words were complaints about a sour smell, much like buttermilk, he said. Some checks were made, but nothing was found, and as pilot he elected to go on with the test.

Next, a high oxygen flow set off an alarm that technicians believed was harmless, but the matter was never really settled. Voice communications deteriorated once more to the point that it became necessary to hold the countdown. The launch team and the crew continued work on the communications problems and were ready to resume the countdown at 6:31 when ground instruments showed a rise in oxygen to the spacesuits. Four seconds later, Chaffee's calm voice said, "Fire. I smell fire." Two seconds later, more excitedly, White could be heard saying, "We've got a fire in the cockpit!" Then, an unidentified voice yelled, "We've got a bad fire . . . get us out. We're burning up . . ." There was a scream, then nothing. Twelve seconds had elapsed.

As a North American Aviation employee waiting in the white room rushed toward the module, it ruptured, filling the air with flames and black smoke so that seeing anything was impossible. Mechanics, technicians, and crews from North American Aviation, all made Herculean efforts to rescue the astronauts but were dropped to their knees by secondary blasts. When some finally reached the capsule, they frantically tried to open the hatch, but the heat was so intense their gloves melted on to the metal, forcing them to retreat. They went back again, trying again, but it was five minutes before they were able to open the hatch, too late. The astronauts were dead. Fire destroyed 75 percent of Grissom's suit, 25 percent of White's, and 15 percent of Chaffee's. The capsule was a total loss, all instruments were destroyed, nothing was salvageable.

The three bodies were left strapped in their seats while investigators pored over the remains, trying to find out exactly what happened. Beside the tragic deaths, twenty-seven other workers were treated for smoke inhalation and two men had to be hospitalized.

As word of the disaster spread throughout the close-knit space community, many employees rushed back, wanting to help. At midnight workers respectfully removed the three charred bodies from the

Apollo capsule after the fire.

space capsule, an occasion like a horrifying death in the family. Other Floridians, especially the thousands who watched space shots from their backyards, grieved.

The grief that spread throughout the country and even the world was soon followed by extensive misgivings about the space program. The respected commentator Walter Lippman wrote a highly critical article in *Newsweek*. Senator William Fulbright questioned "the inflexible, but meaningless, goal of putting an American on the moon by 1970." A *New York Times* editorial castigated "the technically senseless" and "highly dangerous" dedication to the meaningless timetable of putting a man on the moon by 1970.

From then on, when someone on the Space Coast said, "the fire," everyone knew which fire was meant. Heartbreaking though it was for the people of NASA, the fire became a unifying event, a "one for all and all for one" thing that outsiders, no matter how sympathetic, could never understand. One engineer suggested it might have been good, since if it hadn't happened on the pad, it would have happened in space, which would have set the space program back at least ten years. One thing everyone at NASA agreed on was that things had changed. People were more serious, less sure of themselves. It would be some time before any youthful, adventurous attitude returned.

Those involved pointed fingers mostly at themselves. North American Aviation's president Lee Atwood could not believe it when he heard what the test conditions were—"locking those men in a spacecraft, pumping sixteen pounds of oxygen on them, and telling them to operate complicated electrical equipment"—it was so obviously wrong—then.

Chris Kraft, NASA's first flight director, said, "We'd put three astronauts in harm's way and made their escape impossible. They were dead and we knew that it was our fault."

In the meantime a review board avoided accusing anyone directly but did criticize the fact that astronauts had no means of swift escape.

They strongly advised that the hatch be redesigned to allow for quick escape.

NASA did not need to be prompted to give priority to redesigning the hatch. A new one that opened outward with minimum pressure and other safeguards was in the works immediately. Water hoses were added, along with fire extinguishers and a slide wire that could be ridden to the ground in emergencies.

But without the bravery, skill, and true grit of the astronauts, none of it would matter. Moreover, who knew the risks better than the astronauts themselves? Gus Grissom himself once said, "If we die, we want people to accept it. We hope that if anything happens to us it will not delay the program. The conquest of space is worth the risk of life."

CHAPTER 14

THE DE FACTO CAPITAL OF LATIN AMERICA

Mariel to Miami
1980

Things did not go well in Miami, Florida, or in Havana, Cuba, in the 1980s.

On April 1, 1980, a Cuban driver crashed a bus through the fence surrounding the Peruvian embassy in Havana, demanding political asylum. He was followed by ten thousand more Cubans seeking refuge from the island's sinking economy and job, food, and housing shortages, which embarrassed Fidel Castro so much that he ordered the port of Mariel opened for other Cubans who wanted to leave. Many did—and they all headed to Miami.

In another month, one of the most violent racial episodes in Miami's history would explode. Miami, and indeed all of South Florida, would never be the same.

Just as early Jewish newcomers to Miami in past years had faced insulting restrictions, both subtle and blunt, not all Cubans found emigration as easy as they had expected. Still, they came. As did thousands of others from Puerto Rico, Venezuela, Columbia, Ecuador, and elsewhere in Central America. Change had clearly come to South Florida, and it was understood that Miami was the de facto capital of Latin America.

By 1980 many Cubans who had had high hopes for the Castro government were increasingly disappointed politically and economically
and were beginning to empathize with the opinions of their exiled
families and friends. The Cuban economy was at its lowest point in
five years, jobs were scarce, wages were low, the sugar crop was down,
fresh vegetables were hard to find, and rice and meat were rationed.
People had grown tired of feeling constantly watched by police and
frequently having to show identification cards. While life in Cuba had
become unpleasant, family or friends who were living in the United
States told of promising opportunities, financial and otherwise.
Hearing these tales, it was hard not to be envious.

When Hector Sanyustiz, a young unemployed Cuban, learned
that the Peruvian embassy in Havana would not turn asylum-seekers
over to Cuban police, he somehow secured a bus and drove it through
the fenced-off grounds around the embassy. The government of Peru
granted political asylum to the gate-crashers, which included five
other Cubans on the bus, and refused to turn them over to Cuban
authorities. The Cuban government retaliated, announcing they
would no longer protect uncooperative embassies. They withdrew the
guards they had stationed on the grounds and then broadcast over
the radio that people desiring to leave Cuba should proceed to the
Peru embassy. Word spread fast, and by April 6, ten thousand asylum-
seekers had gathered on the embassy grounds, which was about the
size of a football field. Living conditions deteriorated rapidly.

The overwhelmed Peruvian government organized a relief program, as did other nations, which agreed to take some of the asylum-
seekers. President Jimmy Carter, who had been seeking better
relations with Cuba since his inauguration in 1977, said the United
States would accept 3,500 refugees. He welcomed what he called the
"Freedom Flotilla," saying the United States would "continue to provide an open heart and open arms to refugees seeking freedom from
Communist domination."

Castro, embarrassed by the fiasco at the Peruvian embassy, immediately moved to turn the situation to his advantage. He offered to provide asylum-seekers with papers, including passes and passports, allowing them to leave Cuba. On April 21 he announced that the port of Mariel was open to anyone wishing to leave Cuba if they had someone to come by water to pick them up.

When the news reached Cuban exiles in the United States, thousands sped to Key West and Miami docks to charter or rent boats or run their own boats to Cuba and bring their relatives and friends to America. Some boat owners charged a thousand dollars to transport one Cuban the 110 miles back to Key West. In just three days, more than one thousand boats, including pleasure cruisers, motorboats, and others that were little more than rowboats with motors, left Florida for Mariel to pick up those who wanted to leave Cuba.

The U.S. Coast Guard was busy around the clock, coming to the rescue of boats that were out of gas, overcrowded, or not sufficiently seaworthy for the trip. A fierce storm increased the difficulties. Some boats were lost, others overturned, and the Coast Guard carried out the largest peacetime operation up to then, searching for bodies floating all over the Florida Straits. Although the Cuban government ignored their request for names of the passengers and of the boats sailing from Cuba, the Coast Guard continued to keep a close watch out of safety concerns. The U.S. Navy joined them in carrying out air patrols over the waters and by June had activated some nine hundred reservists.

The first week of the Mariel Boatlift saw the arrival of six thousand Cubans in Key West, with about three thousand disembarking there every day for a month. Just one day after Carter's "open arms" speech, he was forced to declare a state of emergency in Florida.

Camps had to be set up all around the Miami area, at a former missile defense site near the Everglades, another at the Eglin Air Force Base in the Panhandle, and some in Miami churches. Some

650 refugees lived at the Orange Bowl until they were moved to a tent city under an Interstate 95 overpass close to the Miami River. As quickly as possible, sites were set up where refugees could be documented before being released to family members already living in the United States.

When the Castro regime took power in 1959, the earliest wave of Cubans who fled their country were mostly middle-class or wealthy landowners and businesspeople who quickly established themselves in Miami. They were followed in the next wave by those hired to work in their U.S. businesses. The third wave, the Marielitos, as they came to be called, were a mixture, predominantly younger males without families, mostly unskilled, and what turned out to be 2,746 criminals, some mentally ill—all considered undesirable.

An offer made by the Carter administration to send two ships to Cuba to evaluate people who wanted to move to Florida was immediately rejected, and the exodus continued. Promising to replace the chaotic boatlift with an orderly one or by use of an airlift, Carter was ridiculed. His reputation had already been plunging—the economy was in a downturn, and an array of crises continued in far-off Iran. The widespread but mistaken belief that all or even most of the Cuban exiles were criminals made their relocation increasingly difficult. Sites needed to house them for longer periods were established in Wisconsin and Georgia, and in Fort Chaffee, Arkansas, where in a short time the exiles rioted. Some broke out into the streets, forcing Governor Bill Clinton to call out the National Guard. His political reputation took a major hit in the midst of a reelection campaign.

In the meantime, Cuban authorities were indiscriminately allowing overloaded boats, some not seaworthy, to leave for Florida. During one six-day interval in May, more than sixteen thousand asylum-seekers arrived. When a 35-foot pleasure boat loaded with fifty-two people sank in Florida waters on May 17, the Coast Guard managed to rescue thirty-eight. They told Cuban authorities that people were dying because of overloaded boats. The Cuban government did not respond.

The Mariel Boatlift reached crisis proportions for both the Carter administration and South Florida by early June. By then more than eighty thousand Cubans had arrived in Key West. On June 20 Carter declared that Cuban immigrants would be allowed to remain in the United States and become "permanent resident aliens" after two years, which would make them eligible for medical and some other benefits. Also, state and local governments would be reimbursed for much of the costs they had been shouldering. It was at least a partial defusing of the growing resentment.

U.S. hopes that Castro would be more amenable to ending the impasse were met with hostility. Nevertheless, the action at Mariel diminished, with fewer and fewer boats engaged. In September, U.S. diplomats journeyed to Cuba, held talks with Castro, and offered plans for improved relations, including increased shipping of food and medicines. The plans were accepted, and on September 26, 1980, the port of Mariel was closed.

Although some refugees were disappointed by the reality of life in the United States, at least half of them wanted to remain in Miami. Some Miamians expected unemployment to rise drastically; it did rise by 2 percent for a short time, but that was comparable to what was happening in other large cities. (Subsequent research indicated that the incoming refugees did not raise unemployment in the long term but actually boosted the prosperity of the South Florida area.)

Crime did rise drastically, however, as Cuban criminals and junkies settled in Miami, which briefly became the "murder capital of the world," although in some cases, without sufficient evidence, police frequently charged newly arrived Cubans, who did not speak or understand English. Most of the Marielitos, however, were hardworking people who lived law-abiding lives and shunned the criminals, who eventually died or were imprisoned or returned to Cuba. As time passed, the crime rate declined.

According to U.S. authorities, approximately 97 percent of the former Marielitos are still located mainly in the Miami area—raising families, working, and paying taxes—establishing a colorful Cuban community. They own restaurants and are doctors, artists, writers. One, Mirta Ojito, is a Pulitzer Prize winner. Another, Gloria Estefan, is a musical superstar. Their pasts may be Cuban, but their future is American.

CHAPTER 15

THIS IS NOT A DRILL

The *Blackthorn* Collision
1980

The unofficial motto of the U.S. Coast Guard, "You have to go out; you don't have to come back," was far more appropriate on the night of January 28, 1980, than its official one: *Semper Paratus* (Always Ready).

None of the *Blackthorn* crew who lived through that night could ever, for the rest of his life, forget the sounds, the ungodly screech, the clank of metal colliding against metal, the tearing of steel, the sudden gush of water, the banging, the shuddering, or the crewmate lurching through the narrow passageway, screaming, "There's an anchor in the crew shower!"

The *Blackthorn* was a 180-foot Coast Guard cutter built in 1943, whose crew was taking her back to her home port in Galveston, Texas, after a four-month overhaul in Tampa. She was a buoy tender; that is, her primary mission was to set and repair buoys. Her age was not unusual for a buoy tender. Many of them serve as long as forty-five years, and she had been renovated and modernized throughout. Among the improvements completed on her were overhauled air conditioning, an upgraded heating and ventilation system, a new

100-kilowatt generator, better crew berths, heads, dispensary, lounge, and a pollution abatement system.

Like other buoy tenders whose duties are frequently diverted to other assignments, the *Blackthorn*'s long years of service included ice breaking on the Great Lakes, searching for survivors of plane crashes and ship capsizings, and salvaging of wrecked Air Force aircraft. Buoy tenders belonged to the "black-hulled fleet" of the U.S. Coast Guard, tugs and tenders and barges whose hulls were black, as were the fingernails of their crews. They set unwieldy aids to navigation into the waters, painted and repaired them when needed, drove pilings—all heavy, hazardous, dirty but important, life-saving work.

The weather that night was almost perfect. The seas were calm, temperature was sixty-one degrees, visibility was good, and there was a light north wind. To someone unfamiliar with nighttime navigation, it might seem incredible that two large ships could collide under such circumstances. However, in darkness when the horizon is not discernible, radar screens can be misleading, and it is easy to confuse navigation lights with lights on shore, bridges, or other ships.

Tampa Bay, the nation's seventh busiest port, opens into the Gulf of Mexico. Ships from everywhere in the world come and go, day and night, passing quite close together at times to keep from running aground while navigating through the various turns in the long channel.

The *Capricorn* was a 605-foot tanker carrying 150,000 barrels of oil from St. Croix to a power generating plant on Weedon Island at the northern end of St. Petersburg. As she prepared to enter Tampa Bay, she was proceeding along in Mullet Key Channel, which is 600 feet wide and 43 feet deep at that point, about to make a left turn at approximately 1 mile west of the Sunshine Skyway Bridge. Her crew was already getting her anchors ready for docking.

Captain George Sepel was present on the bridge of the *Blackthorn*, but a relatively inexperienced ensign, John Ryan, was at the controls.

Disregarding maritime regulations, the captain did not seek assistance from local river pilots for help in guiding his ship through the channels as he headed for the Gulf. Instead, he and his officers, none of whom were familiar with the area waters, maneuvered the ship down Cut A Channel, under the Skyway Bridge, behind a Russian cruise ship, the *Kazakhstan,* which was decorated with many festive lights, and which also may have contributed to the confusion. In midchannel, the *Blackthorn,* going full speed, had just begun making her turn to the right into Mullet Key Channel where the bend was slightly widened but still required great caution from the captains of approaching ships.

The incoming *Capricorn,* temporarily controlled by a river pilot but still under the command of her captain, was also going full speed toward the Sunshine Skyway Bridge and heading on up to Tampa. She was starting a turn to the left, a maneuver which would prevent the ships from passing port to port in the customary procedure. The pilot on the *Capricorn* blew two short whistles, indicating they should pass starboard to starboard. (Port is the left side of the ship, facing forward. Starboard is the right side, facing forward.) He received no answering whistle, but as was later reported, neither ship slowed down. The ensign at the controls of the *Blackthorn* apparently became confused, and instead of trying to communicate with the *Capricorn* by radio or with established navigational whistle signals, he ordered a collision alarm sounded. Disaster was inevitable. Within a few brief moments, the ships collided.

Although it was nearly a head-on collision, no one at first realized the seriousness of the situation. The *Capricorn* received only minor damage, and although damage to the *Blackthorn* was more extensive, it was above the waterline. The real calamity occurred when one of the *Capricorn*'s two 13,500-pound anchors smashed through the *Blackthorn*'s superstructure, ripping open her port side and dragging her sideways and backward. The ships pulled close together momentarily, allowing the 900-foot anchor chain to loosen. As it did, it wrapped around the *Blackthorn* hull, then pulled taut again as the ships moved apart, with the anchor dragging the buoy tender until she capsized, floated upside down, and sank within ten minutes in forty-eight feet of water. Twenty-three of her crew were trapped below decks.

One young crewman, an apprentice quartermaster, would never forget this, his first cruise, the beautiful night, the excitement of his first time at sea. He was below deck when he heard the alarm, followed immediately by the announcement over the ship's PA system: "Stand by for collision. Collision to port side. Stand by for collision. *This is not a drill*." He heard horns, ship's whistles, screeching, felt the ship lurch violently, saw sparks like welding sparks. He and a few crewmates started to run, climbing ladders from below deck, while shouts of, "Mayday! Mayday! Mayday!" pierced the air. Grabbing life vests as they ran, without warning they were slammed against the steel bulkheads as the ship rolled violently. Then, cold water and blackness swallowed them. The next thing the apprentice quartermaster saw was the rudder and the 8-foot propeller right before his eyes and he knew the ship was upside down. He and some other crew members clung to whatever debris they could grab onto in the freezing water, praying for rescue, with their eyes desperately focused on the lighted Sunshine Skyway Bridge, as though it were a life preserver.

It was 8:21 p.m. on January 28, 1980, and the young man had been part of the worst peacetime disaster in the U.S. Coast Guard's history.

The *Capricorn* received only minor damage and suffered no serious injuries, but twenty-three coast guardsmen from the fifty-man crew of the *Blackthorn* drowned that night. Several men who had reported for duty that same evening found themselves trapped in the engine room, unable to fight their way out, while in another compartment, six men who had gathered at the sound of the alarm drowned together in the utter blackness.

The men who managed to escape by swimming through the submerged compartments and jumping into the water felt as though help would never come. Even in Florida the water in January was icy and extremely rough as a result of all the turmoil on the scene. Some of the injured men fought desperately to hang on to whatever floating debris they could find. The water surrounding the scene of the accident was coated with a rainbow of diesel fuel, the air reeking with the overpowering smell. The men instantly became nauseated when they couldn't avoid swallowing the oil in the churning water. Finally, when they were picked up by some fishermen in a shrimp boat, the rescued men gratefully gulped down the fresh water offered them—and threw it up.

Greatly saddened but thankful to be alive, the survivors counted their blessings and worried about their missing crewmates. One of the missing was nineteen-year-old Seaman Apprentice William Flores, who had completed boot camp less than a year before. Seaman Flores and another crewmate tossed life jackets to the men struggling in the water. When the ship began to sink, his friend jumped overboard, but Seaman Flores stayed behind. He pried open a damaged locker door where more life jackets were stored, fastening it open with his belt in order to allow the remaining jackets to float up to where they could be reached by others. He then went below again to assist other injured shipmates. The seaman died rescuing many of his crewmates and was awarded a medal posthumously.

The busy channel had to be closed for three weeks while three shifts of U.S. Navy workers dove on the wreckage. The first group pulled the bodies of the dead from the wreckage. The second retrieved personal effects of the crew, the third brought up ship parts. Closing the channel was costly to the individual ships that were delayed from entering or leaving, but the cost to the Port of Tampa alone was estimated to be in the millions of dollars.

In time it was decided to convert the old *Blackthorn* into an artificial reef. Bill Burchfield, a retired coastguardsman, had the job of

A salute at Blackthorn Memorial Park, located at the north end
of the Sunshine Skyway Bridge.

deciding where the demolition team should place the explosives to sink the cutter. As he was making a final inspection of the ship, he discovered a Bible partly hidden behind a pipe. Its pages were fused together and he could pull it open only at the twenty-third Psalm. The Bible was in terrible condition, but he saved it and turned it over to the Chief Petty Officers Association. After they had it encased in a block of plastic, they passed it on to the U.S. Coast Guard Academy's museum in New London, Connecticut.

Investigations into the causes of the accident were begun almost immediately. After reviewing the facts, the National Transportation Board faulted the commanding officers of both vessels but put most of the blame on the commander of the *Blackthorn* for not properly supervising its young officer on the bridge. The board blamed both ships for not keeping to their side of the channel and for not trying to signal each other for normal port-to-port passing.

The Coast Guard inquiry placed primary responsibility for the collision on Captain Sepel for permitting an inexperienced junior officer to handle the ship in a difficult situation. The junior officer was chastised for not informing his captain of the imminent collision until it was too late for any corrective action. The captain of the *Capricorn* and the pilot on his ship were faulted for not slowing their vessel or sounding signals to determine the intentions of the other ship.

Captain Sepel was issued a "letter of admonition," but he chose to remain in the Coast Guard for eight more years, although he never went to sea again. "I didn't ask to, and they didn't send me," he answered when questioned about it. Concerning the tragedy, he said, "I can't tell you the hundreds of nights of sleep I have lost. Hardly a day passes without [the accident] coming to mind in some way." He accepted a promotion once in later years, but he never agreed with the official conclusion that his ship was improperly located in the channel. To him, if not to anyone else, the location of the debris on the channel floor was proof that he was not at fault. After his retirement he moved to Juneau, Alaska, just about as far as he could get from Tampa Bay and still remain in the continental United States.

Some good did come out of the disaster. The Coast Guard upgraded the training of its officers by establishing a Command and Operations School at its Academy, where a two-week course is mandatory for any officer who will oversee a ship. The course teaches officers to assess risks, such as navigating unfamiliar ports at night, and they "are given full discretion and encouraged to say no if they feel the risks involved are unnecessary."

Range lights, which aid ships to stay inside the channel, were installed in Tampa Bay. Buoy lights were made brighter, making them easier to identify. In addition it became mandatory that incoming and outgoing ships were required to report their whereabouts to the Tampa Bay Port Authority for monitoring.

Blackthorn Memorial Park was established 2 miles from the scene of the tragedy at the north end of the Sunshine Skyway Bridge. A memorial tablet inscribed with the names of the twenty-three coastguardsmen who died as the result of the collision stands in a place of honor. Captain Sepel has been invited to participate in annual memorial ceremonies, but he has returned only once in a private visit, accompanied by his wife.

"It was very difficult," he said. They stayed for ten minutes; there was nothing to say.

CHAPTER 16

COMMUTE TURNS DEADLY

Sunshine Skyway Bridge Is Hit
1980

It was May 9, 1980, just four months after the tragic accident in which the U.S. Coast Guard cutter *Blackthorn* sank and twenty-three lives were lost in Tampa Bay. After the salvage operations were completed, normal commerce resumed in the busy port.

Early in the morning, Captain John Lerro left one of the cottages maintained by the Tampa Bay Pilots Association on Egmont Key, and with a pilot trainee, Bruce Atkins, was taken into the bay in a small cruiser to board the vessel, *Summit Venture*. The freighter, with its Chinese crew, was coming to Tampa to take on 28,000 tons of phosphate rock to haul to Korea. In the light drizzle the two men succeeded in grabbing the slippery rope ladder hanging from the side of the ship and clambered aboard.

They were greeted by the captain of the ship, Captain Liu Hsiung Chu and his helmsman, Wong Sau Ngok, who did not speak English but who would steer the ship, following the directions of Atkins.

Captain John Lerro, a graduate of the Merchant Marine Academy, had piloted 788 ships in or out of Tampa Bay. Atkins had been a licensed ship's master for Gulf Oil for almost four years before he made the switch to piloting. May 9 would be the last day of the month-long observation period required before becoming a member of the Tampa Bay Pilots Association. Piloting vessels over the 43 miles from the Gulf to the Port of Tampa involves navigating through one of the longest and most hazardous shipping channels in the world, partly because of the shallow water and unpredictable weather, but also because the Sunshine Skyway Bridge was built to connect the shortest distance between two points, which positioned the ship channel diagonally beneath it, providing a much more difficult challenge for pilots. One of the Tampa Bay pilots claimed he and his fellow pilots were the "neurosurgeons of shipping."

Experience is highly prized by the Tampa Bay Pilots Association, the average man having had almost twenty years on the job. Candidates for the programs are carefully chosen, then endure rugged training and are closely monitored in at least a two-year apprenticeship before they are permitted to maneuver the huge freighters through the bay. For their exacting, difficult, dangerous, and at times nerve-wracking work, pilots earn about $244,000 a year.

At 6:30 that morning, the 580-foot freighter was on course, moving through narrow Mullet Key Channel. With no cargo and nearly empty ballast tanks, the *Summit Venture* rode high, almost on top of the water. Unexpectedly, the weather began to deteriorate rapidly, until at 7:30 the ship was being pushed around by the sudden squall that struck with explosive high winds. Sheets of rain reduced visibility to zero and rendered the radar almost worthless. It was the worst possible spot to be in when bad weather hit and the bow was no longer visible from the wheelhouse.

They had nearly reached the point where it would be necessary to make about a thirteen-degree turn to the left, into Cut A Channel, which would take them between the main piers and under the center span of the bridge. Certainly, everyone must have been conscious that it was almost the exact spot where the *Blackthorn* sank four months earlier. Lerro knew there was an outbound vessel in an unknown location, and he knew that to stop might cause him to lose control of the light ship in the horrendous winds. He decided to continue on what he assumed was the correct course. He did not know the wind had changed direction and had already pushed his ship off course, light as she was.

He sent a lookout forward to try to see through the rain that was falling at the rate of seven inches per hour, to watch for buoys or anything that would indicate their position in the channel. He ordered another man to stand by the anchor, ready to lower it if necessary, although the experienced captain was certainly aware that a 22,000-ton ship moving through the water at 10 miles per hour needed a half mile to stop.

He gave the order to reduce speed just when he thought they should start their turn to go into Cut A. The squall cleared slightly and Lerro's heart must have stopped when he saw the enormous Skyway Bridge pier loom directly in front of him, and he knew his ship was out of the channel, all 608 feet of it, aimed straight at a pier.

"Double full astern engines, hard port, drop anchors!" He shouted the orders, but he knew it was too late. The collision was immediate. The bridge fell. Lerro saw a truck fall, then a car, and he screamed to the crew to look for survivors while he radioed over channel 16 for help.

"Mayday! Mayday! Mayday! Coast Guard, Mayday! Mayday! Mayday!"

The Coast Guard replied: "Vessel calling Mayday. This is the United States Coast Guard, St. Petersburg, Florida. Request your position, the nature of distress, and the number of persons aboard. Over."

Then, Lerro's frantic voice: "Get emergency . . . all the emergency equipment out to the Skyway Bridge. Vessel has just hit the Skyway Bridge. The Skyway Bridge is down! Get all emergency equipment out to the Skyway Bridge. The Skyway Bridge is down. This is Mayday. Emergency situation. Stop the traffic on that Skyway Bridge!"

The traffic was stopped—too late for some commuters, thirty-five of whom drove straight over the edge to their deaths.

The center span of the Sunshine Skyway Bridge was a steel girder roadway 150 feet above the main shipping channel, with steep concrete causeways. Even in clear weather the main roadbed is invisible to vehicles on the approaches.

On the morning of May 9, when the blinding squall hit, a yellow Buick with four men inside it was behind a Greyhound bus. The driver of the Buick slowed down to a cautious 20 miles per hour, but as it reached the main span, the driver suddenly realized the bus was not in front of him anymore. Instantly aware that something was horribly wrong, he pressed on his brake pedal and stretched his neck, trying to see ahead, but he could see only a vast, black empty space where the bridge used to be. He pressed with all his weight on the brake pedal, causing his car to slide sideways, then halt, a heart-stopping 14 inches from nothingness. The four terrified men escaped from the car and clawed and crawled their way to safety.

A blue Ford pickup truck driven by Wes MacIntire, passed the Buick, and plunged over the edge of the roadway. It fell onto the bow of the *Summit Venture,* and rolled into the water with MacIntire still inside. Luckily, an air bubble allowed MacIntire to breathe until he was able to force the door open and fight his way out of the truck. He clung to wreckage until a crewman from the ship saw him, threw him a line, and pulled him to safety.

Another daily commuter on his way to work had just reached the point where he could see the red aircraft warning lights on the bridge, but suddenly the lights dropped as the overhead structures started collapsing. He slammed on his brakes and immediately began backing off the bridge, and as he did, rolling down his window to shout and wave warnings to approaching drivers. The drivers of three cars and a

One car escapes disaster by mere inches.
FLORIDA PHOTOGRAPHIC COLLECTION/FLORIDA STATE ARCHIVES

Greyhound bus ignored him and unknowingly continued on to their deaths.

Beside the Ford pickup a Chevy Citation with two people inside, a Chevy Nova with one, a Ford Grenada carrying one person, a Ford sedan with two, a Chevy El Camino with one, and a VW Scirocco with two people were all in the water. The Greyhound carried twenty-six people to their deaths.

Search-and-rescue teams from the training program at nearby Eckerd College in Pinellas County quickly launched a full-scale operation, using two boats to haul bodies from the water, then motor to where they had set up a temporary morgue at Fort De Soto Park for the second time in four months. When the team ran out of body bags, they were forced to fasten some bodies onto the swim platform at the rear of the boat without any suitable covers. The team was uncomfortable with the situation, but there was nothing else they could do.

The only survivor, Wes MacIntire, was bruised and bandaged but recovering in satisfactory condition, only to be subjected to a barrage of reporters who wanted the story straight from the mouth of a survivor of one of the worst bridge disasters in U.S. history.

Just four days had passed, when the Coast Guard Board of Inquiry met in Tampa to hear testimony from everyone involved in the *Summit Venture* tragedy. One of the first to testify was the Captain Liu Hsiung Chu, who told the board that the weather turned bad right after Captain Lerro assumed his duties and that visibility was, in effect, zero at the time of the collision. Deputy pilot Atkins stated that in all his years of maritime experience, he had never seen such a sudden and violent storm as the one on May 9. Compelling statements from a meteorologist accompanied by radar records and photographs informed the board that winds were 50 miles per hour or more at the time of the accident.

While the board found Captain Lerro's decision to continue on during the squall contributed to the accident, it also noted that many other contributing factors were completely out of his control. One Coast Guard official said he tried to imagine what Lerro must have felt in the disastrous situation he was in. He compared it to somebody putting a black hood over Lerro's head and telling him to go on and navigate.

Other people were not so understanding. For safety's sake, Captain Lerro's attorney whisked him and his family to a hotel, but the attorney's dog was abused and Lerro's thirteen-year-old son was verbally harassed.

In the tight fraternity of the Tampa Bay Pilots Association, Lerro had been considered something of an outsider. He must have experienced the same pressures as other young pilots who were anxious to avoid being labeled "gutless" by older pilots, a practice said to be not uncommon. Lerro, a former ballet dancer at Carnegie Hall, was accused of being homosexual, an alcoholic, and a murderer. In the

The scene where thirty-five people plunged to their deaths.
FLORIDA PHOTOGRAPHIC COLLECTION/FLORIDA STATE ARCHIVES

bitter public mood of the time, his life was threatened, as was his lawyer's.

In December 1980, a state Board of Pilot Commissioners surprised Lerro by unanimously finding that he acted in a "prudent manner" in his actions during the catastrophe. Other pilots not on the board disagreed, but Lerro was permitted to keep his pilots license. Although he was deeply affected by his role in which thirty-five people lost their lives, Lerro somehow, amazingly, kept a sense of humor, at least some of the time. When he was backing his car out of the lot where the Board had met, he warned a swarm of reporters who were hounding him that they had better duck behind some nearby poles.

Soon after resuming his duties as a harbor pilot, Lerro began to experience some physical difficulties that were diagnosed as early multiple sclerosis, a slowly progressing disease of the central nervous system for which there is no cure. He seriously considered suicide. In time he returned to the University of South Florida, where he earned a master's degree and counseled criminals until he was confined to a wheelchair, then to his bed. For twenty-two years, a day never passed that he didn't remember that other day, that fateful day when thirty-five people died because of the ship he was piloting. On August 31, 2002, at age fifty-nine, John Lerro died.

Almost immediately after the accident, two-way traffic was resumed on the remaining old bridge span, and within fifteen days the channel below was cleared of debris. Meanwhile, as the decision was made to replace the bridge rather repair than it, reviews of construction methods used for both bridge spans revealed that the span that crashed was more poorly built than the other, older span and that inspections by the Department of Transportation had revealed some deterioration of the piers that had not been addressed for more than ten years.

However, the best protected new bridge in the world opened for traffic in 1987, east of the old spans, with 175 feet of clearance and 193 feet at the center, giving ships better maneuverability. With its state-of-the-art design, the new Sunshine Skyway Bridge will withstand winds of 240 miles per hour, with gusts of 290 miles per hour. The channel beneath the bridge was widened from 800 to 1,200, feet and the treacherous turn the *Summit Venture* missed is now farther from the bridge. Bumpers, called dolphins, were erected to protect the bridge piers, structures which Captain Lerro longed for more than once when he recalled the accident.

Before the old bridge was demolished and hauled away in barges, the last person permitted to drive over it was Wes MacIntire, the occupant of the Ford pickup who had gone over the side on that fateful morning. He was accompanied by his wife, and when they reached the top of the bridge, they dropped thirty-five white carnations into the water, one for each person who lost a life in the disaster of 1980.

CHAPTER 17

NEWS FROM LIBERTY CITY

The McDuffie Riot
1980

Unjust arrests. Gun violence. Shootings of blacks with little consequences. Reciprocal killings of police. Police-protected marches for
racial equality. Sadly, none of it is news.

As far back as the late 1890s, Miami was divided into white and
black sections. The section called Colored Town, later renamed
Overtown, became the scene of early clashes between the races.
Records show that blacks were routinely accused of crimes against
whites, but more times than not, whites were cleared of blame even
when accused of taking a black life.

In 1928, after three white police officers were acquitted of beating
a black man to death for reportedly verbally offending a white woman
downtown, they were denounced by the *Miami Herald* and indicted by
a grand jury. One white officer publicly acknowledged that some police
followed a routine when blacks caused trouble: Strip them, beat them,
and run them out of town while firing guns a few times into the air
for emphasis.

As the population of Overtown grew, living conditions deteriorated.
There was no electricity, running water, or indoor plumbing, and the

incidence of communicable diseases and crime continually increased. Some blacks moved west and north of Overtown, to the area that became known as Liberty City. Distressed by the deaths of some of his young church members, in 1929 the Reverend John Culmer, priest at a prominent black church with a history of working to improve the lives in his community, enlisted the *Miami Herald* to join him in a campaign for better living conditions for the blacks in the area.

The result was the first federal housing project built in the district. Encouraged by the *Herald*'s exposé and pressured by President Franklin D. Roosevelt, the Works Progress Administration (WPA) constructed a housing project with running water, kitchens, and other amenities for the blacks of Overtown. Living conditions did improve for some, but blacks still lived in a strictly divided region where unrest grew and movement into white areas was forcefully resisted.

Racial blowups occurred throughout the country in the 1960s, but few made the front pages the way Miami's did in 1968, when Richard Nixon was nominated for president at the Republican National Convention across the bay in Miami Beach. Attempts to bring attention to the frustrations of blacks everywhere inspired rallies by the Black Panther Party, CORE, and other groups, which started peacefully but went downhill into a full-scale riot. A black child was wounded and four black men lost their lives before that riot ended.

No lives were lost in racial disturbances during the 1970s, but feelings of disrespect and abuse grew, as did the perception of blacks that large numbers of Latin American and Haitian immigrants were receiving benefits and jobs that should have gone to them. In those years, Dade County was the setting for thirteen eruptions of racial violence. Then came the 1980s—on May 17, 1980, Miami descended into the most violent racial explosion in its history.

The event had its beginnings in 1979 when, in the early morning of December 17, police spotted Arthur McDuffie, a black ex-Marine insurance executive, volunteer worker, and father, speeding along

North Miami Avenue on his motorcycle. Sergeant Ira Diggs, a white police officer who was parked near an intersection, saw McDuffie slow for a red light, make an offensive gesture toward Diggs, and roar away. Diggs followed, joined by more than a dozen other police officers at speeds of 100 miles an hour until McDuffie finally stopped, raised his hands in surrender, and was forcibly yanked from his motorcycle. At least six, possibly twelve, police officers surrounded and handcuffed him, and the beating began.

It lasted three minutes. Several witnesses, mostly other white police officers, later said the beating looked like a bunch of animals fighting one another for meat. Initially McDuffie fought back, but held down by officers, he soon lay motionless, beaten with nightsticks or steel flashlights, his skull split from front to back, brain swelling out between the bones. Comatose, he was taken to Jackson Memorial Hospital, where he died four days later. The clean-cut ex-Marine was buried a few days before Christmas, his casket draped with the Stars and Stripes.

Officer Bill Hanlon, who later admitted he had handcuffed McDuffie and helped restrain him, stood by while others beat him on the head with flashlights, cracking his skull "like an egg." Hanlon became a key witness, confessing he had led the cover-up by trying to make it look as though McDuffie had lost control and fallen from his motorcycle. He admitted he kicked the motorcycle, smashed McDuffie's glasses and wristwatch, and, with fellow officers, broke the glass on two gauges on the motorcycle. Other officers ran over the motorcycle with a squad car then gouged the road to make it look like cycle tracks.

Although the claim was made that McDuffie's injuries occurred when he fell from his motorcycle, the medical examiner and investigators later said it would have been impossible for a fall from the motorcycle to have split his head with about ninety times the force of gravity. One investigator stated that unless McDuffie had fallen off his

motorcycle, bounced, and hit his head twelve times, the claim of acci-
dental death was a lie. Investigators also noted that the glass-covered
gauges would not have been smashed the way they were had events
happened the way officers described.

One rumor was that McDuffie sped past the police officer because
he had a suspended license and had already been ticketed once for
it. But if that were so, why would he disrespect the officer when he
stopped at the intersection? Question unanswered.

The police department's investigation resulted in nine officers
being suspended, but when four were charged with manslaughter
instead of murder, widespread rage ignited the black community.
Protest marches and coverage in national publications fed the
expanding fury. In an attempt to prevent an explosion, the trial of the
police involved in McDuffie's death was moved from Miami to Tampa.

At the trial, three officers who had been granted immunity testified before an all-white jury that while several of them had pulled
McDuffie from his motorcycle and begun beating him, it was Officer
Alex Marrero who had pulled off McDuffie's helmet, straddled
him, and, with two hands holding either his nightstick or his steel
flashlight like an ax, beat McDuffie's head, spattering blood several
feet away. Marrero testified that he did strike McDuffie, but it was
because McDuffie was trying to take the officer's gun—a question-
able assertion given that McDuffie was outnumbered, handcuffed,
and slipped from consciousness in just a few minutes.

After four weeks, the case went to the jury, which returned its
verdict in two hours and forty-five minutes. It took thirteen minutes
for the clerk to read the verdict that declared all the officers not guilty.

At which point Miami exploded.

It was about 2:30 p.m. on Saturday, May 17, 1980, when the verdict blasted out over the AP wire and Miami radio stations. Shocked
crowds, both blacks and whites, immediately gathered in the housing
projects and parks; by 5:00 p.m. rocks and bottles were flying and

police cars were being overturned and set on fire. Unaware of the dangerous situation, a young white man, Jeffrey Kulp, his brother, Michael, and Debra, a female friend were driving through Liberty City when their car was suddenly battered by flying bottles and rocks. Jeffrey lost control of the car and ran down a seven-year-old black child. Within seconds the brothers were torn from their car and beaten mercilessly for at least twenty minutes. A black cab driver managed to take the child to Jackson Memorial Hospital, while several heroic blacks helped Debra into a cab to escape with minor injuries. The Kulp brothers were punched, kicked, beaten with slabs of concrete, stabbed with a screwdriver, shot with a revolver, and run over by a Cadillac. Michael miraculously survived, but Jeffrey's head was crushed with a *Miami Herald* newspaper dispenser. He became the first fatality of the riot. He wouldn't be the last.

An hour later, three other whites were stoned and brutally beaten near the same spot where Kulp was killed. The violence spread to other black areas of Miami. Before long, three more victims were killed, and the skies filled with smoke from white-owned businesses looted and set afire. White drivers unaware of the news who drove through the area were bombarded with rocks and bottles. A few vehicles with white occupants were ignited while the passengers were still inside. Soon the violence hit black businesses too.

Shortly before 8:00 p.m., about a thousand people gathered at the Justice Center near downtown for a rally initiated by the NAACP with the city's approval. The event started peacefully, with people chatting and singing "We Shall Overcome," but the crowd became increasingly agitated as the news from Liberty City reached them. The fifteen police officers assigned to the event were so outnumbered they stayed out of sight, watching the situation escalate, fed by false rumors. More cars were overturned, soaked with gasoline, and set ablaze.

Governor Bob Graham activated five hundred National Guard troops and imposed a citywide all-night curfew, to little effect. Sales of alcohol and firearms were temporarily banned, and Graham increased the National Guard contingent to 2,500.

A mob smashed open the glass doors of the Metro Justice Building and set fires inside, while others set fires to the nearby Public Safety Department headquarters, where a few police were still working. Fires were also started at the empty state office building across the street. Nurses and doctors reported to Jackson Memorial Hospital to help with the increasing numbers of victims who had been attacked in their cars. The ugly mayhem continued until 10:00 p.m., when large numbers of well-equipped Miami police came on the scene and the crowd began to disperse.

All six operating rooms at Jackson Memorial Hospital were busy for the entire night on Saturday and on Sunday until surgeries were completed and thirty-five gallons of blood secured from the city blood bank. The chief surgeon in the emergency ward, a man with vast experience, was appalled by the ugliness and severity of the beating injuries, skull fractures, and butchering of some patients. Nine other hospitals treated a total of 417 injured people during the three days of the riot.

As the looting and burning spread to other black sections of Dade County, a 3-mile swath of destruction and plundering of businesses in Liberty City continued until early Sunday morning, when there was a welcome lull. Unfortunately, the break lasted only until 10:00 a.m., when the hordes returned to resume looting until businesses both black and white were almost completely emptied.

The Community Relations Board of Dade County held a long meeting on Sunday afternoon with black leaders, police, and government officials, but little was accomplished. While discussions went on inside, the riot continued outside. Three more blacks were shot and killed, but by that time, after three days, the uproar was clearly running out of steam.

When dawn broke on Monday, quiet finally returned.

In the end, eighteen people had been killed, eight white and ten black, and more than one hundred million dollars in property had been destroyed. The McDuffie family received a 1.1-million-dollar settlement. Under President Jimmy Carter, a task force was formed to come up with an economic recovery plan for Miami. The plan did not result in a triumph.

In the coming years, a burgeoning influx of Cubans from the Mariel Boatlift and the arrival of thousands of Haitian immigrants complicated recovery efforts in the black community. Approximately 90 percent of the twenty-two million dollars loaned by the Small Business Administration was made to white or Hispanic businesses, and less than half of those businesses relocated in the riot-torn area.

As the decade closed, some progress had been made in black Miami neighborhoods, but not enough. Today nearly half of Miami's black and Hispanic residents still live at or below the poverty line. And while most white police officers treat blacks with courtesy and respect, episodes of brutality still occur.

The McDuffie Riot changed Miami forever, but life in the city would go on.

CHAPTER 18

A TRAGEDY FOR THE CONSTRUCTION TRADE

Harbour Cay Condominiums Collapse
1981

When completed, the luxury Harbour Cay condominium complex under construction in Cocoa Beach would consist of two, five-story buildings, each with forty-five units and twenty-eight townhouses. Located between State Route A1A and the Banana River, with a superb view of the river, it was expected to be a most enviable address.

Friday, March 27, 1981, was a good beach day—sunny but with a nice breeze from the ocean. Less than a mile away from the beach, workers at Harbour Cay were preparing to finish the concrete fifth-floor slab of the condominium and were looking forward to the traditional "topping off" party after work, with beer and food, then payday and the weekend. The men were in a good humor.

It was a time of new beginnings for one worker, twenty-four-year-old Michael Cresse. He was in the process of moving from his parents' home where he had been living for three months, trying to save money to pay off debts he'd accumulated during a brief marriage, which ended on March 25, the same day he started his new job. Always good at arts and crafts, Michael anticipated fitting in well as a glass worker with the small subcontracting firm, Florida Plate Glass and Mirror.

Like Cresse, twenty-two-year-old Darrell Nowakowski was finishing up the second day of his job, setting window frames. Darrell was the oldest son of a Merritt Island family whose father, Con, owned the insurance agency that insured the Harbour Cay project. Darrell's mother, Carolyn, was spending the day at the family office in a building across the street from Harbour Cay. She was preparing to teach a women's seminar on Saturday on how to cope with crises.

Another worker, Arthur Battle, a thirty-two-year-old mason, had always worked in construction. With a wife and three children to support, he believed it was the best way for him to make a good living for his family. Many of the other men working on the job were roamers, living in motels, working and collecting their paychecks until the project was finished, then moving on to the next job. They were all ready to celebrate T.G.I.F.

It was almost 3:00 p.m. when the concrete was being poured for the fifth and last floor. Then, without warning the building shuddered and an ear-shattering crack split the air. Some workers instinctively dropped their tools and ran or tried to run. One man leaped from an upper floor and crawled to safety. Another tried for the stairs, but he was too late. Less than five seconds was all the time the men had to make an escape from the tons of concrete and steel crashing down on them, five floors of concrete stacked on top of each other like pancakes, with eleven dead men smashed between them and a giant cloud of white dust rising.

Carolyn Nowakowski heard the gut-wrenching sound. She stepped out of her office with a camera and snapped a few pictures of the concrete clouds enveloping the whole construction site before she ran across the street, frantically searching the rubble for signs of life. She and her husband were not entirely familiar with their son's work schedule, and as she searched, she prayed that he was not at the site that day.

Rescue workers on the scene after the collapse.
PHOTO COURTESY OF THE NATIONAL INSTITUTES OF STANDARDS AND TECHNOLOGY

Arthur Battle was one of the workers pouring concrete on the roof when it trembled, then crashed, sucking him into the wet concrete and twisting his legs into the wreckage. A dead worker slammed across his body as Battle's head was immobilized by a steel beam. He struggled fiercely, knowing he faced an almost certain gruesome death, but other workers saw him and with almost superhuman strength, pulled the beam from Battle's head and dragged him to safety.

Michael Cresse's family was unaware that he was working at the Harbour Cay site until they received a phone call from his roommate who wanted to know where Michael was. With sinking feelings they hurried to the scene, asking everyone they saw if they had seen Michael. Finally, when someone said he had seen a young man answering their description walking around, they breathed a sigh of relief, assuming their son was probably safe, most likely helping with the rescue efforts. Still, they wished they could find him in the mass of confusion.

As the dust began to settle, injured workers could be seen all over the site, groaning, bleeding, begging for help. A massive traffic jam formed on A1A, hindering rescue vehicles that were suddenly coming from everywhere, trying to get through to the scene. Workers who had been spared were joined by passing strangers, everyone digging with their bare hands to try to find someone alive.

Debbie Grant, a detective with the Cocoa Beach Police Department, had been having a late lunch with her husband at a local restaurant. She ignored the enormous thump she heard until she was alerted by a dispatcher's call for help on her police radio. When she heard the report about the building's collapse, she rushed to the scene of horror, joining in the desperate search for survivors. As the day went on, Grant had the gruesome task of assisting the county medical examiner identify and tag the horribly mangled bodies hauled out from the wreckage.

By early Saturday 300 volunteers worked, with front-end loaders and heavy-duty cranes, smashing at the five stories of piled up concrete and steel, hoping, but by then not really expecting, to find anyone else alive. Some workers, with nothing better to work with, continued using axes and sledgehammers, but that was slow work as even the regular cranes had difficulty lifting the huge slabs of concrete. Someone notified the Kennedy Space Center, and they sent two enormous cranes capable of lifting 140 tons that speeded the job.

Thirty-six inmates from the Brevard Correctional Institution joined in the physically demanding work of searching. U.S. Air Force personnel from Patrick Air Force Base arrived with sound detection equipment to listen for moans and electrical generators to supply power where it was unavailable. Air Force medics checked bodies, pronounced deaths, and marked the sites where the bodies were found with orange ribbons.

At times, when someone thought they heard a moan, they would yell it out and everything stopped while the rescuers listened, but when all that could be heard was the squawk of gulls penetrating the silence, the work would begin again.

The search was made more difficult because there had been so many subcontractors working at the site, no one could be sure how many bodies were buried in the debris. Volunteers labored nonstop throughout the night with the help of giant floodlights, some workers working until they dropped from exhaustion.

One bone-weary rescuer stopped briefly to catch his breath and wipe the sweat from his eyes, but another man screamed at him, "Get on it! That could be you in there!"

"I guess there's still hope we'll get someone out alive," said Cocoa Beach Police Chief Robert Wicker. "But not much."

The family of Michael Cresse learned the tragic truth about their son when they opened the morning newspaper on Saturday and saw a picture of the wreckage. They recognized without any doubt a familiar pair of sneakers protruding from a pile of shattered concrete. "That's the first we knew," said Michael's father. "We knew then."

At 11:30 Sunday night, Cocoa Beach Fire Chief Bob Walker ended the search for victims. The last body, that of Darrell Nowakowski, had been pulled from the wreckage eight hours earlier, his crushed tool box beside him and his silver watch still working. While much of the rest of the nation was deeply distressed over the assassination attempt made on President Ronald Reagan on March 30, most of Florida and certainly all of the Space Coast residents could think of little else but the Harbour Cay victims, grieving along with their devastated families and friends.

A funeral service was held the following week. Darrell Nowakowski's bereaved father read a psalm and Cocoa Beach Fire Chief Walker paid tribute to the hundreds of volunteers who, he said, were the "real heroes" of the ordeal. "When I received word about the collapse all I had was a small fire department, little resources, and little man power," he said. But help arrived from everywhere. "There

Building before the collapse.
PHOTO COURTESY OF THE NATIONAL INSTITUTES OF STANDARDS AND TECHNOLOGY

were no city limits, no county lines—just a united community effort to try to pick up the pieces.

"My grandfather used to say, 'A determined man with a rusty wrench can do more than a fool with a whole set of tools.' There were an awful lot of determined men and women out on that site."

Amid the prayers for the dead, encouragement for the injured, praise for the rescuers, one question kept intruding. "Why?" Why did the worst accident in the history of Florida's construction trade happen?

Ken Carper, professor of architecture at Washington State University and a specialist in forensic construction, has written that the four common underlying causes of construction accidents are ignorance, carelessness, negligence, and greed. It would seem all four were represented at Harbour Cay.

Two weeks before the collapse, workers reported serious stress cracks, shaped like spider webs, encircling support columns all through the building. Supervisors marked the cracks with yellow crayon then ignored them, the workers said. The men also said the concrete floors were noticeably sagging between the support columns and added that the wooden beams supporting the concrete floors during construction were cracked and bowed. The steel and concrete pilings that are driven into the ground to make up the building's foundation had already failed a test in one area, but the work continued. Workers wanted to remain anonymous to avoid trouble with future employment, but said they were ignored by their supervisors and told the motto in construction is, "Go like hell."

Keeping building costs down makes for higher profits and speeding construction is part of that equation. "People who develop condominiums do it to make money, and they use the most inexpensive workers and materials," said Jeffe Hoxie, a Cocoa architect who was a past member of the Florida Board of Architects. He also stated, "The basic underlying reason why eleven people are dead is pure and simple greed."

As various investigations proceeded, it became increasingly clear that Professor Carper was correct when, speaking of building failures, he said, "Failures seldom result from a single error made by an individual."

Beginning in the late 1970s, Cocoa Beach building inspectors were having a hard time keeping up with the increased pace of construction in their town. When they received the architectural drawings from the Harbour Cay architect, William Juhn, along with the structural drawings of his structural engineer, Harold Meeler, the Cocoa Beach inspectors accepted them, although the drawings differed in critical ways.

Cocoa Beach officials had also started permitting the structural engineers for various undertakings to conduct inspections on their own projects. At the same time they stopped sending design plans to the Southern Building Code Congress for review. Instead, a city engineer, whose speciality was the city sewage treatment plant, was assigned to check the plans, in order to save the city money.

The design for Harbour Cay was determined by two men who were former engineers at NASA, Harold Meeler and Agustus Allen. Allen did the structural calculations from the first floor up and Meeler did the foundation calculations. According to state consulting engineers, Allen's design contained structurally fatal mistakes. The floor was too thin, there weren't enough supporting columns, and the columns were inadequate. There was no solid inner concrete wall to strengthen the structure against high winds, and the structure was not strong enough to support its own weight, let alone the weight added during construction.

Investigations further determined that three unlicensed subcontractors who had never passed any sort of proficiency verification were responsible for the support structure of the luxury building. Then too, the concrete industry, largely unregulated by government, was known to frequently evade the few standards that were in existence. Additionally, county concrete testing and production firms were not knowledgeable about building codes that required tests of concrete poured on construction projects like Harbour Cay. Further, the testing company doing the tests at Harbour Cay was not accredited by the U.S. government's program.

Wynn Cresse, Michael's mother, like many others, was dismayed when she learned the truth about the construction industry. The forty-eight-year-old teacher channeled her grief for her son into a campaign to toughen government regulation of the industry, making appearances before the Cocoa Beach City Commission, the county's legislative delegation, and the Cocoa Beach Trade Board to push for tougher legislation.

"I couldn't believe the way the codes were written," she said. "Here is something as mammoth as the construction industry, and they don't have stringent requirements."

The state consultant investigating the accident came down hard on the designers of the structure, while the investigator for the U.S. Occupational Safety and Health Administration agreed that the design was deficient but believed errors in construction—incorrectly placed steel support bars, for example—were major contributors to the collapse.

Although the architect, two engineers, and two contractors were disciplined as the result of the tragedy, little else changed. The developer was permitted to complete another similar project not far from the scene of the disaster.

Cocoa Beach's senator, John Vogt, a civil engineer, pushed hard to toughen state construction laws, but in the end he was unable to convince enough other lawmakers and no laws were changed.

A Cocoa Beach architect put it succinctly: "You don't legislate greed."

The survivors of Florida's worst construction accident eventually settled out of court for $10 million, ending the largest statewide legal action in Florida's history, two records no one could ever want to set.

CHAPTER 19

FIRE IN THE SKY

The *Challenger* Explodes
1986

After the completion of twenty-four successful space shuttle missions, the general public was beginning to find the flights becoming almost routine. However, it was always different in Florida, home of the Kennedy Space Center, where people paid more attention to news of the launches, stopping to watch the skies, especially along the Space Coast, Cape Canaveral's neighborhood. There, the routine was to pull over if you were in your car, or to just stop whatever you were doing and sort of hold your breath, maybe say a prayer as you followed the trail of smoke in the sky until it disappeared into the heavens and the ground beneath you stopped shaking. Then you relaxed, smiled, and went on about your business. Until January 29, 1986, when all that changed.

The mission that day did stir up more interest everywhere than the previous ones because it had been heavily promoted as a mission that would carry a teacher into space, the first private citizen ever to fly the shuttle. Popularly known as the Teacher in Space, the shuttle was officially called the STS-51-L, the letters and numbers that indicated the year, location of lift-off, and alphabetical order of the flight.

Challenger crew in the White Room before boarding the shuttle.
PHOTO COURTESY OF NASA

The STS-51-L was the largest space transport ever built, and with two women, an African American, and a Hawaiian, it had the most diverse crew ever assembled. Commander Francis Scobee, a former Air Force test pilot, was the veteran of a previous *Challenger* mission. Pilot Michael Smith, a Navy test pilot, was making his first space flight. Mission Specialist Judith Resnik, the flight engineer, had flown on a previous mission and was the second American woman to fly in space. Mission Specialist Ellison Onizuka, a Hawaiian of Japanese descent, was a flight engineering instructor for the Air Force. Mission Specialist Ronald McNair, a physicist from MIT, was flying his second space mission. Payload Specialist Gregory Jarvis was a technical expert from the Hughes Aircraft Company who'd had a satellite launcher named after him. Payload Specialist Christa McAuliffe, a history and social studies teacher, was selected and trained by NASA to teach children from space.

The flight of STS-51-L was originally scheduled to be NASA's first launch of 1986, but the launch date was postponed several times due to launch delays of *Columbia* in December 1985. Weather caused more postponements, then on January 27, a malfunctioning hatch-locking mechanism forced rescheduling until January 28, when at last everything looked good to go for a liftoff at 9:30 a.m. EST.

High winds accompanied the cold front that had passed through Florida's east coast, but even after the wind died down, the temperature fell into the twenties overnight. It would be the coldest day on which NASA had ever launched a manned vehicle. The astronauts, brilliant people all, did not have to be told that it was cold outside, but they were never informed of the dangers that could accompany those low temperatures. Nor were they aware of the two teleconferences that took place prior to the launch involving thirty-four people from the Marshall Space Center, Kennedy Space Center, and the engineers and managers from Morton Thiokol, the Utah company that manufactured the booster rockets for the *Challenger.* The astronauts were never told that the people at Morton Thiokol advised NASA to delay the launch because the unusually low temperatures could damage the rubber O-rings they manufactured. The crew did not know the space agencies, which were under terrible pressure to launch, asked Morton Thiokol to reconsider and the company reluctantly did, finally approving the launch and ending the teleconference at about midnight.

Awakened at 6:18, the crew enjoyed a leisurely breakfast, waved and grinned as they walked from their van to the launch pad, where the temperature was thirty-six degrees at 8:00 a.m. An elevator took them to the white room; from there they entered the orbiter module and were strapped into their seats and waited. Meanwhile, the Ice/ Frost Inspection team carried out three separate inspections, which must have seemed interminable to the seven astronauts lying on their backs.

There had been similar situations during other holds on previous training days, and when Christa McAuliffe's students had asked her what it was like, she told them, "Go borrow a motorcycle helmet. Lie on the floor with your legs up on a bed, and lie there for five hours. You can't read, you can't watch television, you can't have anything loose around. You're strapped really tightly, with oxygen lines and wires coming out of your suit. You can hardly say anything. Just lie there and you'll know how it feels." To a "civilian" it might seem impossible, but Christa, like some of the others, simply fell asleep.

Finally, at 11:28 a.m., the families of the crew, the students from McAuliffe's school, and the hundreds of spectators and media in the viewing sites at the Cape heard the voice of the chief of public information over the loudspeaker announcing the final ten minutes of the countdown. This time it didn't stop. This time there were no holds and the booming voice of Kennedy launch control announced, "Liftoff! Liftoff for the twenty-fifth space shuttle mission and it has cleared the tower!"

With the earth shaking beneath them, the families and spectators in the stands broke into applause and shouts and cheers of, "Fly, baby, fly!" as they followed the majestic ship clear the tower and roar into the cloudless blue sky. Launch control at that point transferred to Johnson Space Center in Houston.

At seventy-three seconds after liftoff, *Challenger* reached 50,000 feet in altitude and was 7 nautical miles down range when one external tank glowed, turned red, and burst into a huge fireball. A cloud of smoke swallowed the shuttle. Captain Smith's last communication to Mission Control was heard: "Uhh . . . oh!"

Stunned families, watching from the roof of the watch control center, stared in disbelief, amid horrified screams from spectators watching the two white streamers of smoke and debris falling to the ground. In the families' viewing area on the roof of the launch tower

Solid rocket boosters explode in opposite directions 76.4 seconds into flight.
PHOTO COURTESY OF NASA

control center, one of Captain Smith's children cried out, "Daddy! Daddy! I want you, Daddy! You promised nothing would happen!"

Following a brief, ominous silence from the public relations officer, Mission Control delivered the next announcement in a toneless voice: "Flight controllers are looking very carefully at the situation. Obviously, a major malfunction . . . We have a report from the flight dynamics officer that the vehicle has exploded. The flight director confirms that. We are looking at checking with the recovery forces to see what can be done at this point. Contingency procedures are in effect. We will report more as we have more information available."

Family members of the crew, having just watched their loved ones disappear forever from their lives, were taken to comfortable quarters as the largest single salvage operation in world maritime history was begun. U.S. Coast Guard and Navy ships headed to the impact area while Coast Guard, Navy, and Air Force planes searched from the air.

Two hospitals were alerted, the smaller, Jess Parrish Memorial Hospital in Titusville, was the local emergency medical facility for NASA, and Shands Hospital in Gainesville, affiliated with the University of Florida, was NASA's official hospital. Both hospitals had drilled at intervals to be ready for space emergencies. At Shands specially trained physicians were called in and remained on call in case there were any survivors. Until launches were completed, the hospital always kept one operating room free and two trauma specialists, two surgeons, one anesthesiologist, and a critical care specialist on hand. Before each launch astronauts' medical records were sent to both hospitals with properly matched blood available. On January 28 the staffs at both hospitals would have been overjoyed to be of service, but their services were not needed.

The entire nation was stunned, but with the exception of the families, nowhere was the tragedy mourned more than in Florida. All of Florida grieved, but especially the people who lived within an area of about 200 miles, who could look up and see the space flights being launched. Shoppers in the JCPenney at the Merritt Square Mall crowded around a television in the store, white-faced, some dabbing their eyes. A young flight instructor with a lifelong dream of going into space was on a routine test flight for Melbourne Aviation at the edge of the restricted area when the *Challenger* blew up, shattering his dream before his eyes.

Boats were not permitted in a sealed off area of the ocean where salvaging efforts were going on, but fishermen who operated scallop boats out of Port Canaveral immediately offered their services. "Anything to contribute," they said.

People wept unashamedly, the tragedy so touched them. An ex-military bugler who was in Cocoa Beach for the launch, sounded the mournful notes of "Taps" at the Cape as soon as he heard the news. A retired NASA engineer who watched the shuttle had a heart attack when it exploded. He was taken to the same Jess Parrish Hospital where they awaited astronaut survivors.

Local bars on Cocoa Beach where Space Center workers hung out after work were silent. People walking on the beaches as far south as Vero Beach started finding pieces of debris. One woman turned in part of a glove with bone fragments in the tip.

In Washington, D.C., the entire Capitol it seemed, was stunned and grieving. The House observed a silent prayer, then adjourned. The chaplain said a prayer in the Senate where two senators, John Glenn and Jake Garn, undoubtedly felt closer to NASA than the others. Garn was the first civilian in space and had been especially close to *Challenger*'s pilot, Mike Smith, who had helped with Garn's training.

People felt there was a special relevance when John Glenn spoke, having had his own brush with death when he was the first American to orbit the earth. "We are a questing people," Glenn said. "We are a people who are curious . . . a questing people. That curiosity, that questing, will never die, because if it does, it seems to me we as a people die along with it. So we try and we triumph, and we try again and we triumph again, and we try again and again and we triumph every time. Then comes a day when we are brought up short, and we must realize that we are fallible, our judgments are not omnipotent. So our triumphs are matched occasionally by tragedy."

Within seventy-two hours of the accident, investigators were already horning in on where the disaster originated. Shortly, they knew that gas had leaked near a seam where two segments of the booster were joined. President Reagan officially appointed a Presidential Commission on the Space Shuttle *Challenger* Accident, transferring control of the investigation out of NASA's authority.

When the *New York Times* published an article that proposed O-ring failure as being the cause of the gas leak, with the headline, "NASA

Had Warning of a Disaster Risk Posed by Booster," the subject was finally out in the open. The commission uncovered enough information to convince them, too, that the O-rings were the probable cause of the disaster. In several closed sessions they learned about the secret tele-conferences during which Morton Thiokol had acceded to the pressure exerted by Marshall Space Center managers. As for the pressures on the managers, there was plenty of blame to go around. Political pressure? A widespread rumor suggested that the Reagan Administration was press-ing for a launch, possibly to hook up with the Teacher-in-Space mission during his State of the Union address. In 1984 the National Education Association endorsed Walter Mondale over Reagan and according to the rumor, Reagan had pushed for the first civilian in space to be a teacher at the same time as his administration was cutting funds for education. The rumor was never substantiated.

Another means of intense pressure came from the press and that was not hard to prove. The media did their goading publicly when the shuttles were delayed, the *Columbia* seven times in twenty-five days. Then came the *Challenger.* When it was delayed four times, the television networks pressed, one announcing, "Yet another costly, red-faces-all-around-space-shuttle-launch-delay." Another network anchor proclaimed, "Once again a flawless liftoff proved to be too much of a challenge for the *Challenger.*" John Glenn recalled hearing a television newscaster ask, "When is that turkey going to become an eagle?" when a flight was canceled. It did have an effect on people working in the space program, Glenn said.

The commission reported to the president in June, concluding that the O-rings were the technical cause of the accident. They did not excuse NASA, however, stating that the difficulties with the O-rings were known and ignored by them for some time.

At the same time the U.S. House of Representatives Committee on Science and Technology started their own investigation, agreeing with most of the conclusions of the Presidential Commission but also suggesting incompetence on the part of managers who gave the go signal for the launch. The tragedy came down to pressure to launch.

Meanwhile, the most extensive salvage operation in world maritime history was being carried out in a search that extended from Cape Canaveral to Savannah, Georgia. In early March the USS *Preserver,* a navy salvage ship, located the crew compartment about 15 nautical miles offshore. The remains were brought up in secret, placed in containers, and taken to Cape Canaveral, where they were analyzed and identified, then flown to the Air Force Mortuary in Dover, Delaware, before being released to their families. Some unidentified remains were buried at Arlington National Cemetery beneath a Memorial on which is carved a poem, *High Flight,* which Christa McAuliffe carried with her on her final voyage and which was quoted by President Reagan in his message to the grieving nation.

High Flight

Oh, I have slipped the surly bonds of Earth,
And danced the skies on laughter-silvered wings;
Sunward I've climbed and joined the tumbling mirth
Of sun-split clouds,—and done a hundred things
You have not dreamed of—wheeled and soared and swung
High in the sunlit silence. Hov'ring there,
I've chased the shouting wind along, and flung
My eager craft through footless halls of air . . .
Up, up the long, delirious, burning blue
I've topped the wind-swept heights with easy grace
Where never lark nor even eagle flew—
And, while with silent lifting mind I've trod
The high untrespassed sanctity of space,
Put out my hand, and touched the face of God.
                                        —John Gillespie McGee

CHAPTER 20

MORE THAN A STORM

Hurricane Andrew Arrives

1992

Florida takes pride in being the state that best prepares for hurricanes, and why not? The Land of Flowers holds the dubious distinction of being the state that has been hit by more hurricanes than any other.

Florida residents have become accustomed to radio and television meteorologists talking endlessly during the hurricane season, from June to November, about "tropical disturbances" that need to be watched. So it was in the summer of 1992 when, by August 1, no significant weather disturbances had formed. Then in mid-August, the National Hurricane Center mentioned a tropical wave moving off the African coast. As the wave became better organized and formed a tropical depression, television weather people somberly reminded listeners to get prepared with extra batteries, jugs of water, plywood, and canned goods. Still, there was not much reaction, although interest did perk up when the disturbance became a tropical storm and was named Andrew. By Saturday morning, August 22, when Andrew reached hurricane strength, packing winds of 75 miles per hour and was steadily moving west, most people scrambled to stock up on emergency supplies. Actually, that was a bit late because by Saturday evening the lines in supermarkets and Home

Depot were long, and some items were running low or were out of stock altogether. But the day was so beautiful, it was hard to believe anything bad was about to happen, and most people sunned and swam in their pools or boated on the calm seas.

When the storm blasted the Bahamas on August 23, Andrew could no longer be ignored. Floridians hurried to board up their windows, move patio furniture inside, and elevate indoor furniture and appliances to prevent water damage.

Reports of horrendous destruction in the Eleuthera Islands convinced all but a few remaining skeptics that Florida was in for a bad one. Although some were determined to "stick it out," roads were soon jammed with half a million people who decided to evacuate. All the major highways clogged with cars, and on the turnpike all lanes headed north, with tolls eliminated for the duration of the emergency.

Wherever there are human beings, there are foolish ones or those who have been "through this before." Because they made it through one hurricane, they assume they can make it through any other. People in one Miami housing complex decided to have a "Hurricane Party." It was probably the worst decision they ever made.

Nearly 1,400 tourists crammed on to a cruise ship in Freeport when it was announced that they were to be evacuated before there would be a direct hit on the island. Reporting on the total panic, one passenger said, "It was like getting out of Saigon."

At least 1,500 pregnant women were hospitalized in South Florida on Sunday. Some were taken to Fort Lauderdale or West Palm Beach, but the physicians at Jackson Memorial Hospital in Miami asked their patients who were due within three weeks or who had high-risk pregnancies to come to the maternity ward during the storm, for safety's sake. An amazed worker at one hospital said, "I've never seen so many pregnant women in my life."

Construction sites were secured as much as possible, booms on high cranes lowered, debris and barricades secured. Concrete blocks and other heavy material on upper levels of high-rises were a problem for which there was no solution.

There were still some people who weren't convinced it was not another false alarm. The meteorologist at TV Channel 4, Brian Norcross, who would become a beacon of sanity and sympathy and support for the Miami area, warned his viewers, "Absolutely, there is no doubt about it, it is going to happen tonight. . . . Friends, it's going to be very, very bad."

Shelters opened and people were advised about what to bring— medicines or other needed medical supplies, for example. For patients who were living at home and on ventilators, decisions had to be made about batteries or generators. Homeless people were herded into shelters before the police and firefighters were themselves ordered off the streets.

Andrew had arrived. Winds increased steadily, slamming trees to the ground by 2:00 a.m., and by 3:30 a.m. the power went out all over Miami. Air conditioners ceased humming, the comforting presence of television was gone, and the total darkness that is hard to conceive of before it happens, enveloped all of Dade County. Portable radios delivered the comforting voice of Brian Norcross, who warned everyone not to try to venture out *anywhere* as the wind was 145 miles per hour, exceeding the building codes. There is no doubt that he saved lives by that admonition alone.

Telephone poles snapped like matchsticks, and pickup trucks, cars, and furniture flew through the air. Hospitals went into their emergency modes, transporting some patients to more secure wards or into center hallways and dining rooms.

At the National Hurricane Center, the radar dome blew off the roof, before the whole roof was gone. The wind gauge showed winds of 164 miles per hour before the gadget was torn off at 5:20 a.m. Homestead Air Force Base wind instruments recorded gusts of 170 miles per hour before they were blasted away.

People who were hunkered down inside their houses lived through the most terrifying experience of their lives. They heard boards on their houses creak, then rip off. They felt interior walls shake and saw roofs collapse as they cowered in bathrooms or inside closets. Glass patio doors shattered as uprooted trees slammed into their houses. People pulled mattresses and blankets over their heads and prayed—people who hadn't prayed for a long time, prayed on that night that felt endless.

The noise was one that no one who'd heard it would ever forget. "Like a freight train," everyone who had ever experienced it said, but it was worse, louder, so loud you couldn't hear anything else, no individual sounds of things breaking, but an awful pressure in the ears that was in itself almost unbearable. You couldn't shout to anyone; they couldn't hear you. With it all there was a sound like a trumpet shrieking, but that was wind squeezing between the seams of doors and either the door held or more likely, it finally blew and the trumpet went somewhere else and started shrieking again.

Torrential rains poured for hours on end, seawater flooded a mile inland, sewers backed up, seeping into the closets where people were hiding, wondering, not knowing what more would happen, how much worse it would get, how much longer it would last. An hour would have seemed like forever, but one terrifying hour passed and then another and another and the horror didn't stop for four long hours. At 7:30 a.m., Andrew made his exit.

People began to emerge from their hiding places to face a new horror, one that would last much longer than the storm. The devastation appeared worse than anyone could have imagined in their wildest dreams. Halves of houses, whole houses were gone. Shattered glass was everywhere, and people were in their nightclothes and bare feet, the same way they had gone to bed the night before Andrew came. Entire neighborhoods and huge live oaks that had grown for centuries were gone. Belongings were scattered for miles.

A survivor surveys the damage.
FLORIDA PHOTOGRAPHIC COLLECTION/FLORIDA STATE ARCHIVES

People who had evacuated tried to return and couldn't find their neighborhoods, much less their homes. There were no landmarks, no street signs; streets were clogged with trees and wreckage so that when cars did begin to move, people had to drive up on what used to be their neighbors' lawns. Pink insulation draped from dangling power lines, people's hair, and palm trees.

The storm surge had reached seventeen feet in places, which meant the ocean waves pounded into neighborhoods a mile from the beach. When the water receded, a barracuda was found swimming in someone's swimming pool.

The entire building where the "Hurricane Party" was held was gone, as were the party-goers. Ninety-nine percent of the mobile homes in Homestead were flattened or gone, along with everything in them. Boats were stacked on top of one another, sometimes blocks away from where they had been tied up at their docks. Cars parked in garages were in the street, nowhere near where they had been left.

The rain had stopped, the sun came out, and it was summer in Florida and there was no water, no ice, no shade, no air conditioning, anywhere. With such widespread devastation, problems escalated quickly, and with the lack of coordinated relief efforts, they escalated again. Police, whose own homes and families were frequently in desperate circumstances and who were working twelve-hour shifts, led rescue efforts, helped dole out food and supplies, even taking food to forgotten migrant labor camps. Some of the people there were illegal immigrants who hadn't eaten for days, but their intense hunger helped overcome their fear of police.

Since the police were occupied with lifesaving duties, looting took a backseat and soon became an ongoing problem. Storm-damaged houses were so easily robbed, many people took to strapping guns and hunting knives to their thighs. Signs spray-painted on walls or plywood window coverings warned, LOOTERS WILL BE SHOT or, LOOTERS, ALL GOOD THINGS HAVE BEEN REMOVED. Stores in malls were emptied of stereos, televisions, designer label clothes, and bicycles. Those looters were arrested when they were caught, but police didn't have the heart to stop bereft parents trying to find some food for their children at food stores. The officers simply admonished the looters and turned their backs.

Governor Lawton Chiles sent 20,000 National Guard troops to Dade County, a crucial assist in maintaining order, guarding stores, and directing traffic. It was a big help, but it was only the beginning. The entire county's water supply was undrinkable. Dazed people wandered about, not knowing where to turn, desperate for water or some relief from the heat. There was hardly any shade because most of the trees were gone.

At about 6:00 p.m., Air Force One landed with President George H. W. Bush and an entourage, including the governor and a state

A satellite view of Hurricane Andrew.
FLORIDA PHOTOGRAPHIC COLLECTION/FLORIDA STATE ARCHIVES

senator. After a stop to look at an uprooted tree and hold a press conference at which he promised help, the president ended his two-hour
visit and flew away.

By the following day the number of homeless people was up
to 250,000, all still without food, water, sanitary facilities, and no
place to lay their extremely weary heads. The Federal Emergency
Management Assistance Agency, better known as FEMA, came
under increasingly bitter criticism. They were accused of being slow,
confused, and totally inefficient, so little help came from that quarter, either. By Wednesday the boss of Dade County's Emergency
Operations Center, Kate Hale, had had it. She called a press conference. In front of video cameras and radio mikes, with tears in her eyes
but livid with anger, she said:

I want this live. Enough is enough. Quit playing like a bunch of
kids. . . . Where in hell is the cavalry? For God's sakes, where are
they? We're going to have more casualties because we're going to
have more people dehydrated. People without water. People without food. Babies without formula. We need food, we need water,
we need people down here. We're all about ready to drop and
the reinforcements are not going in fast enough. We need better
National Guard down here. They do not take orders from me. . . .
I'm not the disaster czar down here. President Bush was down
here. I'd like him to follow up on the commitments he made.

Before the day was out, 30,000 U.S. Army troops were on their
way to Miami and the navy sent ships south loaded with tons of food
and supplies. Soon, crews built enough tent cities to handle 5,000
people. With kitchens, marked with helium balloons, plus mobile
phones and portable toilets, it was a start—only 245,000 more people
to accommodate!

Something good did come out of the tragedy. Floridians were
stunned at their losses, but they quickly realized they were going to
have to depend on themselves and on one another. In South Florida
people from Haiti, Brooklyn, Peoria, Moscow, Puerto Rico, London,
Toronto, and Venezuela came together as they never did before.
People whose houses still had roofs invited strangers to sleep on
their floors. People emptied their freezers and fed neighbors burgers
cooked on their grills. One man drove all the way to Georgia, filled
his truck with ice, drove back, and gave it away in Miami. People in
Jacksonville, Tampa, Vero Beach, and Pensacola filled their cars with
bottled water, canned goods, diapers, deodorant, Band-Aids, and
whatever else they thought their fellow Floridians might need and
they hauled it to South Florida. Musicians Gloria and Emilio Estefan
who were touring, hurried to their home to Miami while the situation
there was still very uncomfortable, to donate supplies, provide good

cheer, and organize a concert that not only raised money for relief, but also raised spirits with music.

Andrew took fifteen lives in Florida on that frightful night, eleven as a direct result of its victims being crushed in buildings. Three others drowned, two who were trying to ride out the storm in boats. It was estimated that 85 others died of storm-related causes by the end of 1993. Homestead Air Force Base was totally destroyed and closed, removing 8,700 jobs from the area. Over 86,000 people altogether lost their employment and 8,000 businesses were destroyed.

There was a long, difficult time ahead. Restoring power was such a huge problem, crews from Florida Power & Light worked around the clock and brought in workers from out of state to help. They managed to restore power to all their customers in structures able to receive it by September 27.

Just as Andrew brought out the best in some people, it also brought out the worst in others. After the looters came the price-gougers and they were almost as unwelcome. Plywood used for patching up houses, which sold for under $10 before Andrew, sold for $20 to $40 after Andrew. Ten pounds of ice sold for $10 after the storm instead of $1.39 as it had before. Generators priced at under $500 prior to Andrew were selling for $2,000 or more. Some roofers demanded outrageous "down payments" and were never seen again.

It was obvious that building codes had failed. Some believed the codes in effect before the storm were good, but the enforcement had been lax. Whatever was true, the South Florida building codes established after Andrew are the most stringent in the United States, proving once again that some good things can come out of a disaster.

Around the nation and even around the world, people watched their televisions and admired the grit of the people who survived the costliest natural disaster in the nation's history. Five short months later, on January 20, 1993, 60 students from the original 130 members of the Homestead High School Marching Band, all of whom had been profoundly affected by Andrew, were invited to the inaugural parade of President William Jefferson Clinton. As the band marched past the new president, he rose, smiled, and applauded them. It was another memorable experience for the teenagers—far better than the night of August 24, 1992.

CHAPTER 21

A HAPPY ENDING

The Great Seabird Rescue
1993

When the residents of the Tampa Bay area awoke to see thick, black clouds of smoke ballooning over their pristine bay on the morning of August 10, 1993, some of them must have said, "Oh no, not again! Another accident in the bay."

This accident was different, however. No human lives were lost, but it was a disaster nonetheless. This time the smoke came from a three-way collision between a 400-foot freighter and two barges, each pushed by tugs, carrying in all a half-million gallons of fuel, petroleum products, and gasoline. One barge exploded with a huge ball of fire, the other gushed its thick, oily cargo. It was an environmental tragedy that threatened beaches, sea grasses, mangroves, and thousands of marine wildlife, with especially ominous forebodings for the fragile sea turtle eggs that were ready to hatch. Moreover, as expected, anything that threatened the Florida environment, also threatened tourism, Florida's leading industry.

At first, offshore winds blew the oil out to sea. But by late that afternoon, the beach at Egmont Key was beginning to blacken with a heavy grease that fouled everything it touched. Egmont Key is a small, finger-shaped island at the mouth of Tampa Bay, with a national wildlife refuge at its southern end, plus a lighthouse, and a few small wooden cottages used by the Tampa Bay Pilots Association to house their pilots while they await assignment to guide freighters entering and leaving the port of Tampa Bay.

The expanding oil slick was a serious threat, but considering the unpredictability of the wind, tides, and thunderstorms, no one could say exactly where most of the malodorous gunk would come ashore. The Department of Environmental Protection was uneasy.

Deep-water oil spills are inevitably compared with the *Exxon Valdez* catastrophe that took place in Prince William Sound in 1989 when eleven million gallons of oil were spilled, or roughly enough to fill 125 Olympic-size swimming pools. Approximately 1,300 miles of shoreline were affected. Although the spill into Tampa Bay was small by comparison, the possible aftermath was of great concern.

The spreading mess threatened the fifty to sixty manatees who lived in the area, as well as countless sea turtles and birds, both wading and diving. Then too, it was the peak of summer when the larvae and juveniles of most valuable breeds of fish and shellfish are at their most vulnerable state. In addition, if the oil reached the sea grass beds and settled, it would get into the food chain. At the same time the roots would smother and die. At first experts believed the nasty smell of the goo would deter most marine creatures and birds from getting close, but before long they were dismayed to see pelicans performing their vertical dives into the oil to get at fish underneath.

Workers tried to install some protective booms, but that effort was unsuccessful. Because of the choppy seas, the tides and the wind rendered them ineffective. Cleanup crews hoped the oil would come ashore on sandy beaches where it would be easier to clean up, and that it would not advance all the way into Tampa Bay where it would jeopardize estuaries and rivers. On August 13 the black, oily gunk began hitting the beaches in massive amounts and before very long so too did oily birds.

Ten months prior to this tragic event, the foresight of one woman, Lee Fox, prevented it from being a far worse calamity than it might have been, in one aspect at least. Nearly one hundred volunteers, under her direction, had trained at the Pinellas Seabird Rehabilitation Center (PSRC) for just such a calamity as was taking place. Unlike some states in 1993, Florida had no mobile oil response unit, but nevertheless, the people trained by Fox were ready. They were joined by 3,000 volunteers who heard about the calamity and arrived from all over the world to work tirelessly for three months. The determined efforts of all these volunteers resulted in an incredible 85 percent of the more than 350 birds brought to them being successfully returned to the wild. In other similar circumstances, the usual percentage of saved birds is 15 percent, so the results for PSRC, which is now known as S.O.S., or Save Our Seabirds, were spectacular and were largely due to the workers being trained ahead of time.

When the oily birds began coming ashore, volunteers at S.O.S. were handling forty birds every hour in the strictly defined procedures. No time had to be lost learning proper procedures; the workers already knew exactly what to do and how to do it.

As each animal or bird was admitted to the center, workers took them to one of the three triage units the volunteers had set up. Each bird patient had a chart started on them, recording among other things where they were picked up so that when the time came for them to be released, they could be returned to their same familiar habitat. They were then checked and, if necessary, treated for injuries and dosed with Pepto-Bismol, to counteract any oil they might have swallowed while preening. The presence of oil on the feathers or skin annoys birds but ingested oil causes internal bleeding lesions and is fatal.

Seriously injured animals stayed in the triage unit, receiving intensive care for twenty-four hours or until veterinarians said they could withstand washing. The washing process was carefully defined, and if not followed, it could leave birds in worse shape than before. It began with cleaning badly soiled spots, then bathing the birds gently with detergent and water that had to be exactly 104 degrees, warm enough to disperse the oil but not injure the bird. Since all the birds were frightened when they were brought in, workers held them gently and spoke softly to them while carrying out procedures that took forty-five minutes to an hour for each bird. Using Dawn liquid detergent, the meticulous volunteers took great care not to break or bend the feathers, which form an intricate web over the bird's body. Then it was rinse, rinse, rinse, because even the slightest bit of soap remaining on the feathers would prevent waterproofing. As the feathers dried, waterproofing returned, almost miraculously.

Next, the birds were placed in heated pens to dry until they could be moved to large communal pens to rest. Those pens had wading pools with waterproof liners and had been built of plywood by some of the male volunteers who felt more comfortable doing that type of work than they did with hands-on care. Volunteers watched the birds closely as they rested and recovered.

For the protection of the birds and of themselves, the workers wore safety clothing with only their faces exposed, a challenge to their endurance in the intense Florida summer heat. Some dedicated workers got very little sleep, working for at least sixteen hours a day. At night, local college students volunteered for the twenty-four-hour "racoon patrols," during which they constantly walked around the rehabilitation area, on alert for devious racoons who tried every imaginable strategy to get at the caged birds.

It took several weeks for many of the birds to recover, but when they appeared to have recovered sufficiently to make it on their own, a veterinarian gave them a final checkup, including blood work. Workers then transported them in pens to an oil-free area in their "neighborhood," and in one last glorious gesture, they were set free.

THE GREAT SEABIRD RESCUE

For the volunteers to watch the bird spread its wings and fly away was the most gratifying part of the no-salary job imaginable.

Beside the actual hands-on work with the animals, volunteers performed countless other chores, not all of them much fun but all very necessary. To prevent disease, teams worked in shifts cleaning the wading, holding, and transport pens. Someone had to procure food and drink for all the animals and for the volunteers who seldom left the premises. The tables where the birds were washed were built at a height to lessen strain on the workers' backs. Those tables, the pens, the wading pools—all were built by volunteers from materials procured by other volunteers. Other supplies—medical, cleaning, and the like, were secured by the truckload by more volunteers. Procter & Gamble and Publix supermarket donated cases of Dawn detergent, and Cellular One donated mobile phones. Newspapers were needed to line the holding pens and they came straight from the source—the St. Petersburg Times Company, which generously donated two and a half tons of their excellent product, although not for the purpose intended when they produced it.

Meanwhile, the oil was washing up on beaches in ever greater quantities, over an ever expanding area. Someone described the slick as having the consistency of old chocolate pudding, but the foul smell was definitely not like chocolate, and as for the consistency, in places the goo was actually thick enough to stop a small boat. Cleanup experts arrived from all over, including South Carolina, Georgia, Puerto Rico, and everywhere in Florida, from Jacksonville to Miami, some brandishing rakes and shovels, others maneuvering long hoses attached to vacuum trucks. Construction machinery heaved huge plastic bags of oily sand onto trucks—hundreds of trucks—and lumbered noisily along the beaches.

Tourism was at a standstill. Actually, with oily beaches, the foul smell, sleep deprivation from the heavy equipment working outside their windows all night, and constantly encountering workers clad in protective clothing that looked disturbingly like space suits, most tourists were fleeing.

The shipping companies involved were paying for the cleanup. They claimed to have spent more than $22 million in the first two weeks, without calculating any payments for damages. Together, they hired an independent firm, Turnabout Services, to handle the more than 700 claims filed against them. Representatives of Turnabout lost no time in presenting checks to victims, many of whom were losing sleep from worry about losing their businesses. Claims came from motels, large and small; the organizer of a major volleyball tournament whose playing field was no longer usable; and boaters whose expensive lines were oil-coated and whose boats needed to be professionally cleaned to be usable again. The owner of a ski school had to close his business for lack of customers, and his equipment and boats also required extensive cleaning. Citizens were rightfully incensed.

Along with indignation came investigations and enlightenment. Few people were aware of how alarming the situation was in Tampa Bay and how fortunate it was that there had not been more disasters. A special report done by the *St. Petersburg Times* spelled it out and it was a frightening revelation. The enormous amounts of hazardous substances passing into the bay; the pilots who guided the freighters and answered to a board, half of whose members were pilots; the fact that the rules regulating incoming and outgoing ships were so simple as to be almost worthless—it all added up to a dicey situation and calls for reform. Interestingly, the *Times* found that no state-authorized pilot had ever lost his license, despite several of them having been involved in some of the bay's worst accidents over the years.

Soon, people learned that Thomas Baggett, one of the pilots involved in the August 10 accident, had a history of being involved in calamities and recklessness, including arrests for drunken driving, several serious traffic violations, temporary loss of his driver's license, and involvement in several maritime accidents. The sixty-three-year-old pilot had recovered from quadruple bypass surgery and wore a hearing aid and glasses, which he was not wearing at the time of the accident.

As Labor Day approached, life in the bay area was returning to normal and the cleanup was winding down. Unfortunately, some city officials, in doing spot checks along the beaches, unexpectedly found more buried oil patches, this, after a layer of sand a foot thick had already been removed. Disappointed but determined, workers returned to remove yet another foot of oily sand; soon, most beaches were declared to be clean.

It took another three years before an arbitration panel was appointed to fix blame for the accident that caused the worst oil spill in Tampa Bay's history. The panel found Thomas Baggett, captain of the phosphate ship, 65 percent responsible for the accident. Charles Chapman, who was captain of one of the tugs pushing a barge, was determined to be 35 percent responsible. The captain of the other tug pushing a barge was excused from blame.

A U.S. Coast Guard report assigned the blame similarly, suspending Baggett's license for nine months, after which he was involved in another accident, and this time, his license was revoked. Chapman received a six-month suspension.

Cleanup costs were estimated to be in the neighborhood of $40 million.

Save Our Seabirds has acquired a new, larger home and continues its rescue work. Lee Fox, who, since the 1993 disaster, has organized the state's only mobile oil response unit, estimates that S.O.S. rescues from 200 to 250 birds each year. She is always looking for volunteers to train and be ready to respond when they are needed.

CHAPTER 22

THE END OF AN AIRLINE

ValuJet Flight 592 Crashes in the Everglades
1996

Saturday, May 11, 1996, was a normal workday for Captain Candalyn Kubeck, the young pilot of ValuJet's McDonnell Douglas DC-9, which lifted off at 8:20 a.m. for a round-trip from the Dallas-Fort Worth Airport to Miami, with a brief stop in Atlanta. With Captain Kubeck at the controls and copilot Richard Hazen beside her, Flight 592 was cleared for takeoff at 2:30 p.m. for the 110-minute trip from the Miami International Airport back to Atlanta in nearly perfect weather.

ValuJet, was one of the four start-up airlines serving southern Florida that had reaped benefits from the closing of Eastern and Pan Am airlines. Like Kiwi, Carnival Air Line, and Air South, ValuJet acquired experienced pilots and leftover airplanes from the defunct airlines. Boosted by low fares and no frills, the upstart Atlanta-based company enjoyed explosive growth, expanding its service to thirty-one cities and its fleet of planes from two to fifty-one in less than three years.

At about five minutes into the trip, Flight 592's flight-data recorder indicated a surge of high pressure at the same time that the pilots heard a peculiar noise, a chirplike sound. Unable to identify it, they checked their instruments, which indicated an electrical failure. Mechanics had worked on a tripped circuit breaker before they left Atlanta that morning, but all systems were working fine when they departed. Captain Kubeck said, "We've got some electrical problem." Then, "We're losing everything. We need to get back to Miami."

Copilot Hazen calmly radioed Miami, but within seconds the fifty-seven-ton jumbo jet, traveling at more than 500 miles per hour, crashed nose-first into the inky muck of the Everglades. Several fishermen who were in the area ducked for cover except for one, Walton Little, who happened to be a pilot. Little used his cell phone to report the accident, and by using the GPS he had with him, he was able to supply coordinates, allowing rescuers to reach the scene of the accident quickly. It didn't matter how fast they got there though; all 110 people on board vanished, the spot where they entered the swamp barely noticeable.

The Everglades, the famous River of Grass, varied from several inches to 5 feet of water on the surface, then had a layer of about 6 feet of muck, 40-feet deep in spots, over a layer of limestone, and below that rock. One wildlife expert suggested that one hundred elephants could easily be hidden in the desolate spot 15 miles from Miami International Airport where the plane went down and no one would be able to detect them. The Metro-Dade Police and Fire Departments were soon on the scene, working with federal, state, and other agencies to tackle the enormous recovery effort.

A flat spread of coral rock near the crash became a command post for the 120 workers on duty each day. It took at least an hour to drive to the area on the narrow, single-lane road, and after three different cars carrying rescue workers swerved off it into the Everglades, it was decided that helicopters and airboats would be the preferable means to convey workers in and out.

Recovery crews searching for bodies and debris faced formidable health risks besides the heat and humidity. Thick swarms of mosquitoes, poisonous snakes, and far from friendly alligators were just the beginning. Sharp pieces of wreckage cut and nicked workers who risked infections from biohazardous matter, including spilled diesel fuel and decomposing bodies and body parts in the relatively confined area. The Metro-Dade Fire Department supplied food and vital drinking water and set up an air-conditioned tent and artificial docks to accommodate working boats. Salvaged pieces of the plane were stored in a special hangar at the Tamiami Airport.

Experts from the University of Miami School of Medicine regularly sampled the mud and surface water to analyze bacteria in it. When they found the organisms increasing rapidly the first week because of decomposition of bodies and the heat, it was decided that anyone entering the site had to wear disposable Tyvex suits, rubber gloves, face masks, and eye protection, with tape to seal everything together. Divers spent twenty minutes in the water, then returned to the decontamination center where they were spray-washed with a chlorine solution before removing their disposable clothing and placing it in a biohazard trash container. Between sessions in the water, workers rested in an air-conditioned tent and replaced body fluids.

One boat patrolled the area with a sniper armed with an automatic weapon and a handgun, on the lookout for alligators and poisonous snakes. Contractors removed refuse resulting from thousands of disposable drink and food containers and hundreds of contaminated garments. Others hauled portable lavatories and gasoline for boats and generators to the site.

The almost daily afternoon thunderstorms that were normal at that time of year in the area increased discomfort and danger when they were accompanied by lightning. Two passenger buses were kept on hand to provide a means of escape, if needed. With twelve-hour to fourteen-hour days added to the mix, men exhausted quickly and some appreciated the counselors made available to treat them for depression.

Within twenty-four hours the media made its presence felt, bringing in twenty-seven satellite trucks and other assorted vehicles, equipment, and workers.

Divers slipped into the black water two at a time, roped together, able to communicate with each other and with the command post by radio lines. They soon found a crater, measuring 175 feet by 60 feet, where Flight 592 had smashed into the limestone, but incredibly, there was no plane, only small pieces, and there were no bodies. A few days later though, they discovered a new crater, measuring 20 by 30 feet, within the first, larger one. Body parts, personal effects, and larger pieces of debris were found within this smaller crater. Refrigerator trucks moved in to hold human remains until they could be hauled to a morgue at a later time.

With the help of sonar equipment, the U.S. Navy found the two "black boxes," the cockpit voice recorder and the flight data recorder, and although the boxes did not solve the mystery of why the plane crashed, they provided more clues. The last words of the pilots could be heard, then voices from the passenger cabin, shouting "Fire!" Then a sound, a whoooosh, then nothing.

ValuJet was sometimes accused of growing too fast, not keeping up with the amenities older airlines considered to be necessities, and in addition much of their work was farmed out to separate contractors. They had no facilities to accommodate grieving families, but Miami International Airport stepped in, opening a private room for relatives to gather, along with several counselors. Metro-Dade Fire Rescue workers recognized immediately that few, if any, lives would be saved and that their mission was to recover bodies.

The fact that it was Mother's Day weekend added to the poignancy and pain. A father, Bret Rugg, had brought his sons, ages five and eleven, to meet the plane bringing their mother home from a business trip. The special day only made it harder. As hopes for survival evaporated, other families shared stories about their relatives who were almost certainly lost forever. Captain Kubeck's mother, Marilyn Chamberlin, would be having the worst week of her life, not only bearing the grief of losing the daughter of whom she was justifiably proud, but preparing to move her own mother to a nursing home. Captain Kubeck's remains were never recovered.

The McNitts, an entire family of five, would never return from their South Florida cruise. Another mother and her daughter, Kim Rennolds, had enjoyed a scuba diving trip together, during which they had strengthened their relationship. They had planned to celebrate Kim's twenty-first birthday on Mother's Day. A Florida vacation was the prize won in a beauty contest by Lisa Pearson, a former Kansas City Chiefs cheerleader. The families of high school sweethearts Linda and Dan Jarvis knew the two were meant to be together. After losing touch with each other in college, they had each married other people before being reunited later in life. The Jarvises were returning from a Caribbean cruise. Laurie and Hamilton Conway were flying to the graduation of their granddaughter, Laura Sawyer, an honors student who would tearfully receive Emory University's highest honor for undergraduates as she remembered her loving grandparents.

Although on television U.S. Transportation Secretary Federico Pena pronounced the airline safe and his statement was reaffirmed by FAA Administrator David Hinson, investigators unearthed thirty-four previous violations in the short life of ValuJet. Some of the more serious ones were inoperative locks on cabin doors, inoperative weather radar, and jammed landing gears. Pena and Hinson both later resigned.

Other disturbing reports about the safety practices of ValuJet began to surface. A passenger on the next to last flight of the doomed plane, the flight from Atlanta to Miami, Pamela Hettinger, ruefully wished she had warned on-boarding passengers when she disembarked that day. She suspected trouble soon after she boarded, she said, because the lights went off when the plane began backing up. The plane stopped, mechanics came and worked, and when they left, the same thing happened again and again, three times in all. When they were nearing the end of the flight, the lights went out again. "A flight attendant had to use a bullhorn to tell people to fasten their seat belts," Hettinger said.

ValuJet's president and CEO, Lewis Jordan, expressed his condolences to the families at a Miami news conference. He also said that the plane, a DC-9, built in 1969, was up to date on its safety inspections. Its engines, Pratt & Whitney JT8Ds, were considered among the most reliable in the airline industry.

A few days later, four buses and a van carried one hundred mourners along the lonely road to within a few hundred yards of the crash site for a private memorial service. They were shown orange markers in the muck where the plane went down. An airboat carried wreaths and flowers and a teddy bear to the site for them. The teddy bear was in memory of the little four-year-old girl who was not on the original passenger list because she sat on a lap and did not require a seat for what was supposed to be a short hop. Rescue workers stood in a solemn line as mourners passed when the forty-five-minute ceremony ended, some of the workers nearly as upset as the families. "I thought I understood the word sadness," said Luis Fernandez, of Metro-Dade Fire Rescue. "I thought I could somehow think of what the families were going through. I couldn't, until I saw them here this afternoon." Some relatives shook the rescuers' hands, others waved their thanks from the bus window.

Within a few weeks evidence gleaned from crash debris, while not conclusive, strongly indicated that fire in the cargo hold that quickly spread to the cabin was caused by the mislabeled oxygen canisters. Evidence also indicated that many passengers died from toxic cyanide fumes from burning panels before the plane slammed into the Everglades.

Already, a dispute had broken out between ValuJet and SabreTech, a company ValuJet often contracted to perform crucial maintenance jobs. In this case ValuJet hired SabreTech to replace oxygen generators on three of its new planes that were housed in Miami. At the same time they provided the maintenance company with proper procedures and warnings about fires, which could be a danger if the canisters were not packed or stored properly. Investigations indicated the accident resulted when the canisters, mislabeled as being empty when they actually contained oxygen-generating chemicals, were also packed in such a way in the cargo hold of the jet that they ignited and burned. ValuJet was not licensed to carry hazardous material and should not have transported the canisters even if they had been labeled "empty," since empty canisters contain a toxic residue.

Planes were not required to carry smoke detectors in cargo holds at that time, so the pilots of Flight 592 were unaware of the fire until it was too late. "Too late." It was a phrase that sadly echoed when the FAA announced in June that all airline cargo compartments would be required to have fire detectors and extinguishers by 2001.

The search for more wreckage ended.

ValuJet was grounded on June 18 until the FAA could study the crash that occurred shortly after both the FAA and the DOT had declared the airline safe. When the agencies announced that there were "serious deficiencies in ValuJet's operation," the airline agreed to ground itself and work to correct those deficiencies. The union for flight attendants publicly stated the airline should not be permitted to resume operations at all or at least not until its management staff was eliminated from its jobs. The union was overruled.

At hearings before the National Transportation Safety Board in November, ValuJet CEO Jordan testified for ninety minutes, emphatically denying a rumor that ValuJet pilots' rate of pay rose in proportion to the number of flights they completed, which would influence their decisions and possibly compromise their judgment. Families of the dead of Flight 592 were present and were silently horrified as they watched a video reenactment of oxygen-generating canisters igniting, and then heard a sound, the sound they heard on the last of the tape from the voice recorder—a whoooosh.

ValuJet resumed operations on a smaller scale after a forced fifteen-week shutdown, but criticism of the company's safety procedures affected its bottom line and the bottom lines of other low-cost airlines who were cast in the same light in the public's eyes. ValuJet Chairman Jordan bought $66.3 million stock in AirTran Airways, combining the two airlines into one and switching to the AirTran name, but, nevertheless, remaining under strict scrutiny.

SabreTech closed its Miami facility in 1997, continuing business in Phoenix but eventually ending that also.

In July 1996 a funeral service for the forty-nine victims who remained unidentified was held in Miami. Forty-nine black caskets were buried side by side in a single grave. The names of all 110 victims were read as 110 roses were placed one by one in a large vase.

In 1998 families and friends of the victims of Flight 592 gathered for a ceremony 15 miles west of the Miami International Airport to dedicate a new memorial of masonry, stone, and steel columns, designed by members of the University of Miami School of Architecture. At last the families had a place to remember the loved ones who died in the worst air disaster in Florida's history.

CHAPTER 23

RED TIDE STRIKES AGAIN

Manatee Population Decimated

1996

In the first week of March 1996, the dead bodies of Florida's favorite mammal, the manatee, a rotund vegetarian with a homely, but cute, face, began washing up on the beaches and floating in the waters that had been its home for an estimated forty-five million years. Being warm-blooded creatures, it was not unusual for manatee deaths to increase during winter months, and the winter of 1996 had been an abnormally cold one. But the numbers of recorded deaths continued to mount until 236 of the beloved animals were dead statewide, from January to April. That meant that almost one-tenth of the known population of the gentle creatures were dead and no one knew why.

The outbreak began with one dead carcass washing up on an island just north of the well-known vacation spots at Captiva and Sanibel islands in Charlotte Harbor. By the next day there were two more. Then another and another and another. Animal pathologists examined each body. The procedure, which took three-and-a-half hours, consisted of cutting through the blubber, dissecting the organs, and obtaining tissue samples. Dr. Scott Wright, director of the Florida

Marine Research Institute pathology laboratory, and his overworked colleagues were puzzled.

Attempts at finding the cause of the epidemic focused on three possibilities: a biological toxin such as the one that causes red tide, a disease caused by a bacteria or a virus, or a contaminant, such as a pesticide. Other state agencies assisted in trying to solve the mystery and were joined by federal and private groups. The institute sent tissue samples to experts all around the country.

The preponderance of animals with inflamed lungs and airways led some scientists to suspect pneumonia, possibly linked to the unusually cold winter. Some were concerned that if the disease were caused by a virus, the free-swimming manatees could easily spread it to other animals as they moved out of their winter shelters, some of them traveling north, others south. The toxin that emanates from red tide was another possibility, as was the ever-increasing pollution or the changes in salinity of the water from record-setting rains. The problem was that there were many possible causes; but no proof pointing to a particular one. The deaths of the huge, lovable animals continued.

Finally, the weary animal pathologists at the Florida Marine Research Institute, who had been having the dead manatees trucked to their facilities in St. Petersburg, temporarily moved their laboratory equipment to Sanibel to be closer to the catastrophe. Instead of working in modern, air-conditioned facilities with equipment designed to handle the giant corpses as they did in St. Petersburg, they performed necropsies on flatbed trucks, assembly-line fashion, in a barn, with the bodies handled by forklifts. There was also an urgent need to find a way to dispose of the carcasses that would have been cremated had the work been done in St. Petersburg. In time a landfill business willing to bury the bodies was located.

Scientists from all over the world joined in trying to solve the mystery, examining tissue samples sent by the institute. Still, the findings from necropsies were inconclusive. In general there were some

Florida's favorite mammal.
PHOTO © PATRICK M. ROSE, COURTESY OF SAVE THE MANATEE CLUB/WWW.SAVETHEMANATEE.ORG

microscopic lesions on the brains, and normal stomach contents, the latter suggesting the deaths were quick. The same could be concluded from the normal amount of body fat found in the animals; it would have been less if manatees died slowly. The most notable changes appeared in the inflamed mucous membrane of the nasal passages and in the rest of the respiratory tract on down to the lungs, which were also inflamed and scarred.

Throughout the epidemic, public interest was intense. Everyone, it seemed, wanted to help. Some did. Boaters who came upon dead carcasses helped by hauling them to where they could be picked up by authorities, and in doing so, saved the Marine Patrol time and effort. When other citizens reported sighting dead manatees, those bodies could be retrieved more quickly and examined before putrefaction set in, which would render them useless as far as ascertaining any useful information from them.

Some people wanted to help but didn't, inadvertently making false reports of sightings that turned out to be overturned trash cans or dead dolphins. Others offered their unsolicited opinions about what was causing the disaster. Someone suggested that mercury might be leaking from World War II submarines sunk offshore. Another thought since manatees were called sea cows, perhaps mad cow disease was the culprit.

Telephones rang off the hook at any organization even remotely connected to the ocean or to manatees. Concern for the gentle, blubbery creatures heightened as media attention to their plight mounted. In the meantime scientists worked around the clock, trying to solve the mystery.

Though the manatee had existed for millions of years, interest in them among people outside their normal habitat in Florida had been uncommon until recent years. Florida is "home" to manatees, but in summer they go "on vacation," as far north as South Carolina and as far west as Alabama. There have been a few sightings in Virginia and Texas in warm months, but these are rare. Florida manatees are West Indian Manatees and they grow to be from 10 to 15 feet long, many weighing from 800 to 1,200 pounds. Having no natural enemies, manatees are thought to live as long as sixty years.

They are comfortable in freshwater or in saltwater, and as air-breathing mammals, they rise to the surface every few minutes to breathe when swimming. When resting, however, they take a breath just once every ten to twenty minutes, closing nostril flaps in between breaths to keep water out of their nostrils. When not simply swimming, manatees spend most of their time eating. They are herbivores requiring about eighty to one hundred pounds of sea vegetation every day to maintain their enormous size.

Devoted manatee mothers nurse their babies for one to two years, keeping them close beside them during that time and actually placing their own bodies between their babies and whatever they think might harm them.

Before 1996 the first comparable calamitous event recorded by scientists on the Gulf Coast occurred in 1947 when thousands of dead fish littered the beaches and the air was fouled with a noxious gas. Scientists determined the cause of that episode to be red tide, a naturally occurring phenomenon throughout the world, but one that can have catastrophic consequences.

In 1982 the first well-documented manatee mortality event was associated with red tide. The Florida red tide is caused by dinoflagellates, one-celled organisms commonly called "algae," which increase in number to a point where there are several million of the cells in each liter of seawater, and their bloom of yellow, green, or red discolors the water in an area for many square miles. As these harmful algal blooms (HABs) move on toward shore, fish kills and respiratory illness in humans follow.

The damage doesn't stop there. Consuming contaminated fish is believed to have caused death in large numbers of dolphins, particularly during an episode in 1987 when 700 dolphins were found dead. When bivalve shellfish, particularly mussels, oysters, and clams contaminated with the HABs are consumed, humans can become ill. Even without ingesting contaminated seafood, humans are affected when the wind blows toxin particles into the air, causing coughs and burning eyes, nose, lips, and tongue. These annoying but temporary symptoms usually disappear within twenty-four hours after the sufferers move away from the area.

The extraordinary media blitz reporting on the epidemic of 1996 overwhelmed the tranquil facilities at the marine laboratory. Calls came not only from Florida's own newspapers and television stations. The BBC called from London, and *Inside Edition* and *People* magazine posed questions for which scientists had no answers.

After a few frustrating weeks, there was a brief lull in the manatee deaths, during which scientists cautiously hoped the disaster
was coming to an end, but then another dead manatee washed up
on shore, and then another and another, and the disaster resumed,
claiming sixty more animals in the next three weeks. While scientists
doggedly investigated in their labs, other efforts at solving the mystery involved government airplanes patrolling the area, on the lookout
for live manatees. When the animals were found, their location was
radioed to other scientists who were policing the waters in boats and
who sped to the locations, netted the manatees, and drew blood to
test while the gentle creatures must have wondered what in heaven's
name these strange beings were doing to them.

Then finally, in May, after three weeks during which everyone
involved held their breath, no more carcasses turned up, and the
Department of Environmental Protection declared the catastrophic
episode over, though the cause was still undetermined. Investigative
work proceeded amid collective sighs of relief. During a visit to the
area by Secretary of the Interior Bruce Babbit, he pointed out that a
tenth of Florida's existing manatees died in four months, and "when
you get a 10 percent die-off, that is really cause for alarm."

More than one hundred scientists continued their research, ruling
out some previously suspected viruses and bacteria, but still there was
no conclusive evidence pointing to the real culprit. Dr. Scott Wright,
director of the Florida Marine Research Institute's pathobiology lab,
believed there could be more than one cause.

Finally, in early July Dr. Wright made the announcement everyone
had been waiting to hear. "The investigation led us to the unavoidable
conclusion that a biotoxin was the culprit in this event," he said. The
toxin released by those tiny organisms that color the sea during a red
tide also affected the nervous systems of the manatees who consumed
them in the sea grasses they ate. The manatees suffocated because
they were unable to hold their heads out of the water to breathe and

their diaphragms were paralyzed. Scientists thought the mysterious purple lesions on the lungs of some might have resulted when manatees inhaled the organisms as they were eating vegetation. Combined with the unusually cold weather, the fate of so many manatees was sealed.

Mystery solved. But, what to do about it? The epidemic, while alarming to environmentalists, also had a huge economic impact. The estimated loss to the state of Florida was about $40 million. Included in those losses was lost revenue from fish and shellfish. Recreational fishing and boating were hurt, as were restaurants and seafood markets. Resort hotel and tour reservations were canceled and property values in some areas dropped.

Because of the enormous impact of red tide on the economy and on public health, control of it was an urgent concern. That it is a natural occurrence that originates many miles offshore would seem to make control of it impossible. Some scientists thought it might be feasible to release huge amounts of freshwater from Lake Okeechobee through canals and into the Gulf, thus diluting the saltwater that red tide needs to survive. The big unknown there would be what effect that would have on other sea life. Other experts suggested herding manatees temporarily into safe areas when red tides occur.

Though in the end, 151 deaths of manatees were blamed on red tide, marine scientists reminded us that there were 264 total deaths of Florida's favorite mammal in 1996. Sixty were killed by boats, ten in floodgates and canals, forty-two from cold, and the others of unknown causes. Barring natural disasters, boats with propellers are by far the manatees' worst enemies. Establishing no-wake zones, enforcing regulations, fines, and providing education are all vital to the survival of manatees. A special manatee license plate has supplied funds to support all these efforts.

Red tides in the meantime are increasing in number and size of affected area, with central Maine to south of Cape Cod having been subjected to a recent severe outbreak. The outbreaks are becoming more intense and are lasting longer. Further research continues to examine a possible link to contaminants such as pesticides contributing to the bloom of red tide. Some believe better sewage treatment and a decrease in the agricultural use of fertilizer might make a difference in the amount of runoff. Phosphate mining and the sugar industry have come under closer scrutiny as dolphins and coastal birds, too, have been victims. Even overfertilizing of residential lawns might be faulted.

As scientists and environmentalists work and worry, the population of humans in southwestern Florida continues to increase despite ever more frequent red-tide blooms in the Gulf of Mexico. Ear, nose, and throat specialists in that area report steadily increasing numbers of people complaining of cough, nasal irritation, and eustachian tube congestion caused or exacerbated by red tide. Some residents state that after living in the area for thirty years, it has never been so bad. Coughing, sneezing, choking, and the recurring necessity of burying dead fish are common complaints. People with asthma and the elderly are advised to stay indoors, which in Florida may not be what people want to hear, but many say unequivocally, it beats shoveling snow.

Time and again, Floridians have supported measures to protect their beloved giant. Hopefully, it is not too late.

CHAPTER 24

PREDICTABLY UNPREDICTABLE
WEATHER STRIKES

Killer Tornadoes
1998

Florida does not rank high on the list of states frequented by tornadoes. They rarely strike the Sunshine State—except in June, July, or August—are generally brief, not very destructive, and are almost never deadly. The few stronger, more violent ones that have taken place all occurred in the spring. South Florida's most vicious tornado struck Miami on April 5, 1925, killing five people. When a turpentine factory was hit in Duval County on March 30, 1939, four workers were killed. The deadliest northwest tornado that struck near Milton on March 31, 1962, killed seventeen people.

Florida is, however, one of the most hazard-prone states in the United States. With its rapidly increasing influx of new residents, many of whom choose to live in highly vulnerable areas, it is inevitable that natural misfortunes—hurricanes, wildfires, tornadoes, floods—will have an enormous negative impact on the state.

In 1998 the Florida Division of Emergency Management officials wanted to initiate a program to educate the public. They scheduled a tornado awareness campaign to be conducted before the start of the tornado season. People, they felt, needed to be reminded that a tornado watch means conditions are right for a tornado to form, while a tornado warning means one has been sighted. Citizens should know that if they haven't had a warning, their best clue that a tornado was approaching was a telltale rumbling sound. They needed to be instructed on what to do when the National Weather Service did issue a warning; that is, they should take cover in a small room on the lowest floor, away from doors and windows. They should be told not to try to outrun a tornado in a car but instead take cover in a nearby ditch or culvert. Schools all over the state planned to have a drill during the week to familiarize students with lifesaving procedures to follow in the event of a tornado. The long-planned statewide tornado drill was scheduled for the morning of February 25.

But on February 22, Mother Nature, in the form of El Niño, the giant warm puddle of water that undulates across the Pacific Ocean about thirty times every century, tossed the rules out the window and turned the laws of weather forecasting into an exercise in frustration, reminding Florida who was boss. As one expert said, "Thanks to El Niño, Florida weather has become predictably unpredictable."

The National Weather Service knew trouble was brewing as early as Friday, February 20, reporting, "El Niño is running full bore." A Weather Service meteorologist in Melbourne, Scott Spratt said, "The atmosphere was primed for this type of event."

The National Weather Service issued its first tornado watch at 2:00 p.m. on Sunday, February 22, then issued others at intervals throughout the day, to remind people that conditions were right for tornadoes to form. "The storm prediction center has issued a tornado watch for portions of northern and Central Florida and adjacent coastal waters effective this Sunday night and Monday morning from 9:00 p.m. until 3:00 a.m. EST."

Still, there was nothing to be done, and people went to bed as usual on Sunday night.

Not many people owned the inexpensive little NOAA Weather Radios, with receivers that emit alarms day or night whenever severe weather warnings are broadcast. Florida's old tornado alarm system originally constructed for conveying civil defense alerts had proved to be inadequate as a tornado warning. It had been abandoned long ago because it could not be heard except by people who were outdoors.

It was nearly midnight on Sunday, February 22, when most people were asleep that the tornado watch turned into a tornado warning and screaming winds slammed into four counties, Orange, Osceola, Seminole and Volusia, in what would be the worst day of tornadoes ever to hit Central Florida. The few people who were awake to hear the bulletin on radio or television had less than ten minutes to act. In that amount of time, there was little they could do. So much lightning flashed through the sky, it was almost as bright as daytime. One man said his house was lit up so brilliantly, it woke him from a sound sleep even before he heard what sounded like a jumbo jet.

That was just the beginning. From Disney World, near Orlando, to Daytona Beach, 75 miles eastward, calls for help poured into emergency centers. Trailers were pitched into the sky, some collapsed, others were shredded. The tornado that touched down near Interstate 95 in Volusia County blasted four tractor-trailers off the highway, overturning and scattering the enormous rigs like toys. Docks and piers that lined the dozens of lakes in the area were ripped away and landed on roof tops.

Survivors would later remember and try to describe the night of fury by the sounds, either a freight train, a jumbo jet, or a thousand whistling tea kettles, and by the smell of gunpowder that they wanted to forget but couldn't. The black hole in the sky with lightning flashing all around it, tore across the land, destroying everything in sight.

It was not just one tornado. Three of them hit Winter Garden, a suburb of Orlando where the Country Gardens Apartment complex was heavily damaged. Joe Saz, a resident, recalled it this way: "You could feel the whole apartment just shift. It jumped to the right. Suddenly, water started coming out of the walls, out of the light fixtures, and there were screams coming from every direction."

As always, mobile homes took the worst beatings. Three people were killed at the Hyde Park Mobile Home Park in Orange County. Josephine and Ned Woods found identifiable scraps of their retirement home when they searched through the rubble for her medicine. "It's all gone," Mrs. Woods cried. "This was our whole life. I'm seventy-three years old and you can't start over at seventy-three . . . I wish it would have killed me."

Even some well-built homes were leveled or blown off their foundations. A pickup truck was impaled on the roof of one home. Substandard pavement peeled from roads and flew away. Trees snapped, large ones were uprooted, the bark of others was stripped off.

In Osceola County a man herded his young daughter to the center of his house just before the tornado blasted it and sucked the girl out of his arms. He was badly injured and had to be hospitalized. The battered body of a little girl fitting the description of his daughter was later recovered in area woods.

Judy and Manuel Rincon had saved ten years for the house where they hid in terror, watching it disintegrate as they clung together with their daughter. Then the kitchen door tore away, nearly tearing five-year-old Elissa away too, but her mother held onto her by her legs. "She was horizontal, and my wife was holding onto her legs," Manuel said. "There was all this glass, and everything started to disappear, all the furniture, the insides of the walls. If my wife had let go of Elissa, we wouldn't have been able to find her." But the mother did hold on and Elissa did not become one of the deadly statistics.

The town of Kissimmee in hard-hit Osceola County was the scene of the night's worst casualties. Ponderosa Park, a tourist campground on the outskirts of Kissimmee, was filled with campers who had not yet departed from the Silver Spurs Rodeo that had been held on

Tornado devastation at Hyde Park.
FLORIDA PHOTOGRAPHIC COLLECTION/FLORIDA STATE ARCHIVES

Sunday and the incoming fans of the Houston Astros whose spring training had just begun at their home in the Osceola County stadium next to the park. Almost all of the ninety RVs in the park were tossed about, with a body from inside one flung all the way to the Florida Turnpike, 100 feet away. A sixteen-year-old girl was blown out of a window 150 feet into a pasture.

The campground was a mass of rubble, homes upside down, on top of each other, some wrapped around debarked ponderosa pine trees with cars, shattered glass, sofas, and sinks scattered about.

Rescuers who brought in bloodhounds to search for bodies in the rubble were sickened by the smell of leaking propane gas while they listened for the sound of weak voices calling for help. Tracking survivors was made more difficult because many of them were "snowbirds," part-time Floridians with no permanent Florida address, and also because so many records and files had been scattered.

Manuel Rincon was luckier than another young father who had been clinging to his eighteen-month-old baby boy in his mobile home near Kissimmee. That child was torn from his father's arms and the small body was found seventeen hours later in a tree. Another young couple had been asleep with their one-year-old daughter between them when the ceiling fell on them. They all crawled out, three grateful survivors, only to find the Cadillac they had parked in their driveway had disappeared.

Mark Price pushed his fiancée, Jennifer Johnson, into a closet of their trailer that was too small to hold both of them. He held her hand as the "freight train" came closer, but when it arrived, it tore him from her grasp and he vanished. Neighbors found Jennifer running through the night, calling for Mark, whose body was found later.

Sheriff's crews searching the devastation in helicopters spotted a man clinging to a small boat in nearby Lake Harney, in obvious need of help. They radioed men on the ground, who then motored out and pulled Freddie Padgett from the water, injured but stable. Officers learned that Padgett was deathly afraid of water and always wore a life jacket to bed when storms were predicted. He had it on Sunday night when his RV was destroyed and he was sucked into the St. Johns River, then washed into adjoining Lake Harney, where he was found clinging to a boat.

Several men from Rod's Fish Camp on the St. Johns River were tossed into the river with their trailers when a tornado swept through. Joel "Lucky" Heaton, a roofer, was among them. Some of the missing men were found in local hospitals, but Lucky remained on the missing list until March 2, when his body, clad in blue jeans, was pulled from the river and officially identified, the last of the forty-two deaths from the tornadoes.

It was determined that winds of 260 miles per hour had accompanied the 75-mile-wide path of devastation that pounded Central Florida, leaving more than 250 people injured, whole neighborhoods turned into piles of rubble, more than 3,600 homes destroyed, and an estimated $36.8 million in damage. As always, there were heroes whose names will never be known, but there was no shortage of people helping people.

Janice Sandberg made a substitute ambulance out of her truck, hauling ill and injured people through the dark night and fallen debris to where paramedics could treat them. Students from the Florida Christian College near the Ponderosa Park rushed to comfort survivors and help in any way they could. A man who lived nearby, Gary Stephens, lost part of his roof and a barn but counted himself lucky and went to work with his chain saw to clear fallen trees in order to make moving about easier. Children who lived in the paths of the tornadoes endured an experience that traumatized adults emotionally, so it was not surprising that many youngsters were fearful and upset afterward. Jackie Lilly, a woman of Port Orange, started a drive to collect 1,000 teddy bears, knowing how much comfort children can derive from cuddling them. Lakeland High School students started a drive to get necessities for victims of the storms. In Kissimmee more than 300 volunteers joined others in Operation Umbrella, working on leaky roofs to spare the strangers who lived under them any more problems with the rains that remained in the forecast. The sister of a woman whose leaky roof was being patched by strangers said, "I will never say I hate people again. You don't realize how many good people there are."

Governor Lawton Chiles toured the area on Monday and was stunned at the devastation. "I thought I'd seen everything when I'd seen Andrew, but this is Andrew revisited," he said, promising help from the state. Two days later, President Clinton arrived, touring the area by helicopter, then on foot through the Ponderosa Park Campground, promising to do "whatever it is within our power to do" to help the survivors.

As the cleanup continued, some facts became clear. There were at least seven tornadoes that blasted across Central Florida during that horrible night, causing 42 deaths and 260 serious injuries, and none of the deaths occurred in frame houses. Thirty-one deaths were in mobile homes, ten in parked recreational vehicles, and one in a car.

It had been known for some time that 16 percent of Florida housing consisted of mobile homes and that mobile homes are "very vulnerable to any tornado," as stated by Paul Hebert, head of the National Weather Service in Miami. "They destroy them," he said. "They lift them up and throw them through the air." Some mobile home parks have shelters on their grounds for emergencies, but when another state tried to pass legislation requiring all to do the same, the mobile home industry rose up and managed to block the laws.

After Hurricane Andrew, federal laws were passed mandating stricter standards for mobile homes, including a requirement that they be able to withstand winds of 110 miles per hour. Commendable standards, but in truth 90 percent of the nearly 1.2 million mobile homes in Florida were manufactured before the law passed. Mobile homes built after 1976 were only required to withstand winds of 90 miles per hour and those built before 1976 had no restrictions at all. In an investigation by the *Orlando Sentinel,* it was learned that more than half of the destroyed or badly damaged homes in Central Florida's 1998 tornadoes were built before the 1976 standards were enacted. Although the new standards appear to be effective, the sad truth is that it will be a long time before the older, less-safe homes are eliminated. In the meantime the majority of people living in mobile homes are those least able to afford moving into newer, safer ones.

CHAPTER 25

FLORIDA ABLAZE

Summer of Wildfires
1998

After experiencing a winter so wet Floridians expected to see Noah float by on his ark, April 1998 turned out to be one of the driest Aprils on record. Still it hardly seemed possible when the Division of Forestry issued a wildfire alert. Reports that a fire cut the Keys off from the mainland for five hours sounded like a bad joke. Unfortunately, it was not.

Many parts of the state had had almost no rain since March. Florida became so parched by May that even her swamps were drying up. Over the Memorial Day weekend, 108 wildfires were reported, the biggest of them was the 1,200 acres in the Apalachicola National Forest, where heavy machinery and fire trucks were off limits. To fight the blaze a plane carrying 2,000 gallons of a flame-retardant solution headed to the area, as did more firefighters from New Mexico and Nevada.

The fast-moving fires ignited brush as they swept through Putnam and Seminole counties and on into Flagler County, where some people had to be evacuated, then on to St. Johns County, near St. Augustine, America's oldest city and a precious historical gem. Parts of the east

coast's main north-south highway, Interstate 95, had to be closed
because of the thick smoke hindering drivers' visibility. As reports
continued to pour in, Lake and Brevard counties joined the unfortunate list of those with fires, although theirs were contained for the
moment. "We've got a rural area with a lot of underbrush that's dry as
a bone and it's just feeding the fire," cautioned a representative from
Flagler County Emergency Management.

By the following Sunday morning, Seminole County residents
who had been evacuated on Saturday were escorted by police back to
check on their homes, fifteen of which had been destroyed. Flagler
County declared the brush fires there were out but not before losing
twenty-three homes. Citizens quickly formed committees to organize
a relief benefit concert and collect money and badly needed clothing.
The survivors meanwhile straggled between the homes of friends and
motels with their children and the few meager belongings they had
managed to save, as they tried to find some place to live.

Temperatures climbed to ninety-eight in Orlando, one hundred
in Daytona Beach, and set records all over the state. Combined with
the dryness, a U.S. Forest Service representative proclaimed that "the
entire state is a virtual tinderbox."

About 500 people, half the population of the little town of Waldo,
near Gainesville, had to be evacuated when afternoon winds blew the
fires to within 5 miles of their homes. When the blaze got uncomfortably close, the U.S. Navy pulled 600 of their people out of Cecil Field
Naval Air Station, a jet base near Jacksonville. The city of Jacksonville
was forced to issue a ban on all landscape watering as the result of
water pressure dropping below the volume needed for firefighting.

Florida Agriculture Commissioner Bob Crawford urged people
to refrain from doing anything that might cause fires and to report
all suspicious activities. Some fires were set deliberately and arrests
made quickly when perpetrators were caught. "I cannot even begin to
think of what possibly can be in the minds of those who would set the

woods ablaze and cause so much harm and grief for so many people," Commissioner Crawford said.

As record high temperatures scorched people all over the South in May and June, senior citizens were advised to seek air conditioning wherever they could find it. Miami firefighters had an unusual problem to deal with when toasted local folks pried open fire hydrants to cool off in their sprays. The water couldn't be spared nor could the firefighters, who had fires to fight, use their precious time to close off the hydrants.

Already, farmers estimated losses in hay, corn, and soybeans to be at least $75 million.

Record heat continued, increasing people's misery. Caused by lightning and fanned by winds, thirty-five wildfires broke out in Volusia County. Local firefighters were grateful for the help they got from crews from North Carolina and Tennessee, but the helicopters that assisted from the air had to be grounded when thick smoke buried the airport and wiped out pilots' visibility. Flying tankers that carried 400 to 500 gallons of fire retardant were also stranded. "If we crash an airplane or hurt somebody, we are no good to anybody," said a reluctant spokesman for the Department of the Interior, which had organized the operation.

On the rural land below, people kept a sharp eye on the direction of the wind to help them decide how to safely move their animals. Cattle ranchers had a difficult time moving their animals away from the smoke and intense heat. Dogs and cats were not much of a problem, but moving horses was difficult, even with trailers, which often sank under their heavy weight into soft, sandy back roads. One woman had been caring for her vacationing neighbor's horses but was unable to get them out when fire surrounded her. Tearfully, she prayed for their safety.

Another woman moved her children to safety, then returned for her horses but was stopped by firefighters who advised her to leave them. "I couldn't," she said, tearful but determined. "I've had one for eighteen years." She ignored the advice of the firefighters and somehow managed to move her horses to a secure area.

Many churches and schools opened as shelters for people. The Volusia County's Emergency Management and Animal Control departments opened an animal shelter at the Volusia County Fairgrounds where large animals, including two pot-bellied pigs and several goats, were taken. Several ranches also made their facilities available at no cost for larger animals and horses, an invaluable service to some grateful people.

One man near Daytona Beach wrestled with a unique problem, "wrestled" being the key word. Eddie Colosimo pushed and tugged his five 150-pound emus from their pen into a trailer to move them to a safer locale. The birds, who can run 30 miles per hour, had other ideas, however, as attested to by the bloody marks all over the victorious Colosimo's arms.

By late June, as weather forecasters were predicting the hot, dry weather would continue, every county in the state but one was declared a disaster area. Just three inches of rain had fallen in Florida where twelve was normal. When fires were considered under control, they would unpredictably flare up again, exhausting firefighters, and the general populace who evacuated, returned, and evacuated again, sometimes two or three times. No one disputed the official who said, "This is a very trying time."

While flames seared the land, the heavy layer of smoke wreaked havoc on the atmosphere. The very old, the very young, pregnant women, and people with respiratory ailments were warned to stay indoors, in air conditioning, if possible. People whose homes were not air-conditioned were advised to spend time in malls and theaters or go to air-conditioned shelters. Because of liability, people on oxygen could not be accepted in shelters and were sent instead to overburdened hospital emergency rooms.

As billions of tiny pieces of burned matter slipped through air conditioning filters, sore, raspy throats were the order of the day. Drug stores did booming sales in cough drops, eye drops, and paper masks, though doctors said masks were not very effective. Hospitals treated an increasing number of patients for shortness of breath.

Railroads had to be rerouted in some instances because of acres in flames near the tracks. The Sea Ray boat company had to close because of smoke in the plant, as did a movie theater complex. More importantly, seven of the seventeen firefighting aircraft at the DeLand Airport had to be grounded because of poor visibility due to smoke. The possibility of midair collisions increased with the number of working planes in the sky.

Aircraft had been playing an increasingly important role in fighting the inferno that spread over so much of the state. In one type of operation, helicopters with huge buckets slowly descended to about the height of treetops and released their water. Other flights by single-engine, fixed-wing tanker planes sometimes dumped water but also carried a chemical retardant, colored red so it was visible to the pilots. It stuck where it hit and was very effective in stopping fire from spreading. The chemical was nonhazardous and disappeared when rain finally did arrive. Both methods were used.

One unusual two-engined helicopter was brought in all the way from Oregon to help in the effort. The strange-looking crane resembled an insect and could suck in 2,600 gallons of water at one time, an effective addition to the firefighting arsenal.

Bulldozer crews and other personnel from the National Guard, and the U.S. Forest Service and firefighters from Virginia, North and South Carolina, and Virginia arrived to help. Since the blazes were so widespread, there was competition in the state for both crews and heavy equipment as the heat, smoke, fires, and grit took their toll. "It's getting old," one worker said. "Get about six hours of sleep and the next day come right back out here and sweat again." Another man in

Fire on State Road 11, near Bunnell.
PHOTO BY LIZ ROLL, COURTESY OF FEMA

the protective gear that locked in the heat, swiped at the ashes stick-
ing to the sweat on his face and wondered aloud how much more he
could take.

Everyone had high praise for the Salvation Army, which supplied
1,200 meals and drinks every day to firefighters and emergency crews.
Its staff worked with volunteers to cook meals and make sandwiches,
then drive them to wherever they were needed. Restaurants contributed by supplying meals, while other businesses and private indi-
viduals donated supplies. Gatorade, a Florida invention and a most
effective aid in maintaining correct body fluids and electrolytes in the
intense heat, was passed out everywhere.

Although many Fourth of July celebrations around the state were
canceled, it was announced that the Pepsi 400 race at the Daytona
International Speedway would go on. The first primetime live race, it
was expected to shatter attendance records and be a huge boost to the
Central Florida economy. Firefighters from all over the country who
were being housed in Volusia County and Flagler County hotels were
going to have to leave to make room for the incoming fans, most of
whom had reservations made for at least a year in advance. People in
the area felt bad about it, but hotel managers insisted there was nothing they could do, signed contracts were binding. Firefighters were
less upset than anyone. They were used to it, they said, if worse came
to worst, they would sleep in tents. Local citizens joined authorities in
finding accommodations for them in auditoriums, school gyms, empty
model homes, and private homes. A crisis was averted.

By June 28 the 1,000 firefighters in Volusia County were able to
say for the first time that all major blazes were contained in what was
thought to be the worst outbreak of wildfires in the nation. The state
of emergency would not be lifted until fiery conditions improved—
the high temperatures, the wind, and only a slight chance of rain could
change everything again in a hurry.

As Lieutenant Governor Buddy McKay thanked firefighters in the Daytona Beach area, Senators Bob Graham and Connie Mack toured by helicopter and pronounced the Volusia fire Florida's worst ever. Vice President Al Gore arrived in Daytona and met with officials and private citizens, collecting information to relay to the president.

The wisdom of the officials in not lifting the state of emergency became apparent when on June 29 a wildfire thought to be contained caught a shifting wind, ignited the dry roots of some trees, and roared into Brevard County, necessitating the first mandatory evacuation issued there since the conflagration began. Several businesses and a group of mobile homes went up in smoke an uncomfortably short distance west of Cape Canaveral. Authorities were forced to close a stretch of Interstate 95, naming Brevard County the state's newest hot spot and reporting a dramatic increase in new blazes. Two days before summer's biggest holiday, 125 miles of I-95 had to be closed as embers from old fires were being blown by 15 mile per hour winds to new spots, starting fresh fires. By nighttime all roads except State Route A1A were closed. In Ormond Beach a sheriff's helicopter had to pick up fifteen people who were trapped and carry them to safety. By 10:00 p.m., 300 mostly older patients were evacuated from the Emory L. Bennett Veterans Nursing Home, some confused and frightened by all the lights, noise, and other hubbub. As the areas of mandatory evacuations grew, so too did the numbers of shelters that opened. A special one for people with special needs, staffed by a physician and seven nurses, was set up in a high school.

Driving presented a special set of difficulties for motorists, what with heavier than usual numbers of people trying to find safety and roads blocked by smoke. People could hardly believe it—would it ever end? Weary firefighters couldn't believe it either.

Instead of celebrating the Fourth of July in the customary way, one young couple in the small town of Bunnell decided not to be discouraged by the fact that the official who was to marry them had left town because of the fires. They asked Bunnell's police chief, Flynn Edmonson, who was certified to perform marriage ceremonies, to do the honors. He did, fittingly clad in a Jimmy Buffett shirt, on a wedding day memorable for many reasons.

Officials decided to postpone the Pepsi 400 race until October, which was the final blow to the devastated economy in Volusia County. With thousands of acres of timber gone and the summer's biggest weekend wiped from the calendar, clearly, losses were in the millions. As the fires once again came under control, people were allowed to return to their homes, if they were still there.

The reactions of survivors of what is thought to be the nation's worst wildfire ranged from tears of despair from one woman to the quiet resignation of her neighbor. "It's just stuff. It's all replaceable." One man who lived alone pawed through the ashes of heirlooms left to him by his mother, finding a bowl his mother used for his scrambled eggs when he was a child and his mother's chandelier. A family returned to their destroyed home, unsurprised because they had watched it burn on television, knowing it was their home because of the familiar trampoline in the backyard.

On July 9 President Clinton visited Daytona Beach. He praised firefighters who came from all over the country and other workers, promised federal help, plugged Florida tourism on national television, and said, "Maybe it shouldn't require a disaster like this, but you did show our country at its best. . . . I hope it's something we never forget."

CHAPTER 26

AN UNFORGETTABLE HURRICANE SEASON

Hurricanes Charley, Frances, Ivan, and Jeanne

2004

Full-time Florida residents expect the annual summer ritual of after-noon thunderstorms and daily warnings about specks on the map off the coast of Africa that could turn into something but rarely do. The predictions of long-range forecasters in early June of 2004, however, had an ominous sound to them. A meteorologist and innovator in long-range forecasting, William Gray, led in predicting a worse-than-average hurricane season, with the possibility of four major hurricanes for the east coast and the Gulf coast. Gray and other forecasters agreed that while the powerful hurricanes had turned away from the southern coast in recent years, the area was due for some bad ones. A meteorologist from the AccuWeather weather-forecasting company predicted trouble in particular for the Gulf coast and the National Oceanic and Atmospheric Administration joined in, anticipating an active season.

One reason why more hurricanes were expected to form over the Atlantic Ocean was that hurricanes draw their energy from warmer water and the water there was slightly warmer than it had been a decade earlier. Most meteorologists believe it is part of a weather cycle that has been going on for very many years. Gray agreed with that, adding that warmer water corresponds to the increased salinity of the water, part of a cycle that lasts for decades and is unrelated to greenhouse gases or other human-created conditions.

In early August a tropical storm that forecasters had been watching turned into a hurricane that swept western Cuba and was expected to pass west of the Florida Keys on Friday, August 13, before zeroing in on the Tampa Bay area later that day. Named Hurricane Charley, the sneaky fellow changed his mind and aimed squarely at Lee and Charlotte counties at the same time as he exploded into a devastating category 4 storm. The Keys and the entire west coast of Florida were put under a hurricane warning, which meant that almost two million people were advised to evacuate. The advisory included Tampa Bay and St. Petersburg and all but essential residents of nearby MacDill Air Force Base, the location of the U.S. Central Command and official center of the war in Iraq.

While heavy traffic clogged highways out of Florida, residents who remained behind boarded their homes and stocked up on water, nonperishable food, and batteries. Power companies mobilized their workers and made arrangements with out-of-state companies in preparation for the onslaught of outages sure to come.

It was just before 4:00 p.m. when Charley smashed into North Captiva Island with 145 mile per hour winds and ten-foot waves, the first powerful storm to hit there in forty years. Winds of 180 miles per hour slammed Punta Gorda, the small town in Charlotte County to the north that was hardest hit. Charlotte County, claiming the nation's largest percentage of senior citizens, was home to more than thirty trailer parks with hundreds of elderly residents. Because the voluntary evacuation advisory had so quickly and unexpectedly turned into a mandatory one, officials knew it was going to be difficult to assess casualties.

Making a ferocious entrance, Charley flattened homes so fast that within a few minutes it appeared as though hundreds of them had never existed. Some houses piled on top of other houses and trailer parks instantly converted into huge trash piles, precious remnants of people's lives strewn about with the debris. The fifteen-foot storm surge pushed boats up onto the land on Pine Island, where downed power lines sparked a wicked fire that burned out of control for more than an hour until fire trucks were permitted onto the barrier island.

Charley moved fast, clobbering the mainland at about 4:15 p.m., peeling the roofs from part of the hospital, schools, airplane hangers, and a shelter housing 1,200 people.

"Happy Friday the thirteenth," one man grimly wished everyone at 6:30 p.m. when it was deemed safe enough for survivors to go outside, survey the damage, and begin learning to live with the consequences of Charley's visit. In the intense heat and humidity, they would need all their strength to endure long lines for water, ice, gas, food, and government aid. There was no power and so, no air-conditioning, no refrigeration, and no lights after dark.

As Lee and Charlotte counties began their recovery, Charley continued on his way across Central Florida, passing through Orlando before heading out to sea at Daytona Beach. The narrow, fast-moving hurricane left thirty-three dead and a mountain of destruction behind.

A few weeks later, just as Florida was preparing to celebrate the long Labor Day weekend, the National Hurricane Center began making ominous noises again. "Warm air masses" and "Doppler radar" and "tropical depressions," they were muttering, and Floridians knew it was time to start preparing for another unwelcome visitor. This latest interloper was named Frances, and she was a creeping Amazon who affected nearly the entire state, moving so slowly, it would take her three days to cross the peninsula. Holed up in boarded-up homes, shelters, or motels, residents had more time than usual to prepare— that was good—and more time to worry—that was bad.

Maybe it was because less than a month had passed since their neighbors on the west coast lived through the mess of Charley, or maybe it was that Frances was a very impressive 400 miles wide, but this time more than 2.5 million people from Miami north to Flagler County jammed airports, Florida's turnpike and Interstate 95, eager to comply with the state-ordered evacuation of twenty-one counties. Many left the state in the largest evacuation in Florida history.

As the interstate highways more and more resembled slow-moving parking lots, drivers on the whole remained surprisingly civil. Tempers did occasionally flare as in one ludicrous incident on Interstate 4 when two tractor-trailer drivers stopped their trucks in the middle of the highway in a fit of road rage. Gawking drivers backed up traffic in both directions, unable to believe their eyes. Fortunately, a sheriff happened along, jumped from his vehicle, shouting, "Y'all have any idea that the entire coast of Florida is evacuating and you're stopping traffic to fight?"

Coast Guard planes searched the waters, ordering any lingering vessels to return and tie down at whatever dockage they could find. Luxury cruise ships kept passengers safe by cruising south for a few days, well away from the storm, rather than anchoring anywhere near its path. "Out of harm's way in a resortlike setting," one company official bragged.

Meanwhile, the residents of the Treasure Coast got ready for their first major hurricane in more than fifty years. Hotel telephones nearly rang off the hook with prospective guests canceling the plans they had made for the big holiday weekend. Adding to the general confusion, the rooms were quickly snatched up again by folks trying to escape the destruction of Frances. The problem was that no one knew just where to go or how far to evacuate.

Hospitals on the coast moved patients to safer locations, while those farther inland prepared for the onslaught of evacuees being transferred to them. Most ordered extra blood supplies and scheduled their staffs to be on call to work extra hours.

Drug stores frantically tried to fill the extra prescriptions people ordered, some handling two or three times the usual number for customers preparing to ride out the storm. A dog-lover in the Orlando area endured standing in a long line for a sedative prescription for his pet greyhound who, he said, went ballistic in storms.

Leading television journalists and news anchors moved into the area, prepared for a major story. Young meteorology students from Florida State University in Tallahassee arrived at Fort Pierce, driving their specially equipped car, hoping to capture Frances on videotape. Residents who had prepared as best they could and were beginning to get cabin fever, just wished the slow-moving storm would get a move on.

Frances considerately downgraded herself to a category 2, with winds of 105 miles per hour by the time she finally came ashore about 1:00 a.m. on September 5, at Sewall's Point on the east coast, 40 miles north of Palm Beach. Winds of 105 miles per hour can still do much damage and Frances did, bashing yachts into docks and into each other at the Fort Pierce City Marina, ripping out power lines to leave millions without power and sparking unauthorized "fireworks" displays. Pouring twenty inches of rain in some localities, flooding was inevitable in low-lying areas, including the first floor of the Indian River Memorial Hospital and the sheriff's office in Vero Beach. At least two tornadoes touched down, felling trees, blocking roads, and hindering emergency crews. So little time had passed since Charley's visit, there was no time to pick up all his lingering debris, which then turned into missiles launched by Frances.

At one mobile home community in Port St. Lucie, residents gathered in their clubhouse, a hurricane shelter. They waited out the storm munching popcorn and watching a movie—*Gone with the Wind,* wishing the wind they were with was gone.

State Route A1A, the main highway running north and south along the barrier islands, was littered with street lights, parts of roofs, and business signs, and was made completely impassable in some places by fallen trees and light poles. Salt and sand, two or more feet deep piled up inside beachfront houses, but even homes built some distance away had roofs and walls torn off, kitchens and bathrooms exposed to the world.

Frances crawled through Florida at just 7 miles per hour, dragging out unimaginable miseries, most residents wishing she would do what she had to do and get it over with. Her leading edge hammered the coast early Saturday, shutting down much of the entire state, including airports and amusement parks for the normally busy Labor Day weekend.

Water damage due to missing roofs and from high water affected buildings from the mobile homes in the poor town of Pahokee in western Palm Beach County all the way to Donald Trump's lush estate on the Palm Beach shore. Not far from the famous Worth Avenue, the rabbi at the Temple Emanu-El had wisely sent the temple's ten handwritten Torahs to a bank vault for safekeeping, but the temple's library, the third largest Jewish library in the state, was soaked.

Florida farmers who knew in a very short time that their losses would be catastrophic, estimated them to be $3 billion in an industry that generated more than $6 billion revenue in 2003. Ranchers found their cattle coping with water up to their bellies, while farmers tried to rescue some of the tons of their citrus crop that floated beneath the trees of their groves.

The usual long lines circled for blocks around stores, as desperate people searched for water and ice. More lines formed at gas stations, but supplies of gas were low because tankers that would replenish them were waiting offshore until the threat of hurricanes was out of the picture.

Big, slow Frances, a category 2 hurricane, took three days to get herself across the state and finally leave with thirty-seven dead and an enormous mess behind.

While people were still reeling, trying to repair damage from Frances and get their lives back in order, a new hurricane, named Ivan, was lashing Jamaica with pounding winds and torrential rain. The U.S. Army Corps of Engineers was scheduled to install blue tarps on Frances-damaged roofs all over the Treasure Coast but was pulled back because of Ivan. Generators needed to pump sewage promised by state and federal governments were not delivered because of Ivan. Storm-weary Floridians muttered, "Ivan? Here we go again," as they hauled themselves off to restock supplies once more. Incoming trucks kept resupplying home improvement store shelves that customers swept clean as fast as they were filled, buying items to repair damages from the past storm and to prepare for whatever was coming.

Florida's emergency management director described Ivan as possibly the worst storm of the year, a "complete storm," with significant to catastrophic storm surge, significant to catastrophic flooding, significant to catastrophic winds, and possible significant to catastrophic tornadoes.

As Cuba was being whipped by Ivan's hurricane-force winds, Fidel Castro announced that his nation would not accept help from any countries that imposed economic sanctions against his country. "The United States can save itself the hypocrisy of trying to help Cuba out of this situation," he said.

Ivan, a category 4, crashed ashore at 2:00 a.m. around Mobile, Alabama, right next door to Pensacola, where 130 mile per hour winds crumpled piers and washed over the barrier islands. Pensacola was on the eastern side of Ivan, the right front quadrant, where hurricanes pack their strongest force. Bulletlike rain shot horizontally across abandoned streets, while a buoy in the Gulf of Mexico registered waves 50 feet high.

The shelter at the University of West Florida filled quickly, as did the one at the Pensacola Civic Center where shelter manager said, "I'm not planning on turning anyone away. But I'm not sure how close their cheeks will be."

One elderly couple refused to leave their home on Santa Rosa Island even when twenty-five-foot waves pounded the barrier island and all bridges closed that afternoon. The couple was never seen again. Four city hospitals were badly damaged, but no one was killed there nor in a nursing home where the roof was torn off.

The storm surge of sixteen feet drowned four people, sent one family to their attic when the van they had been hanging onto floated away. A pickup truck landed in a luxury swimming pool, and 70 percent of the homes in the affluent neighborhood were demolished.

The disaster at Pensacola's beach could be described only as catastrophic. Hotels with shattered windows, roofs ripped off, ground-floor areas washed with salty water, and sand several feet deep, would be out of business for many months and some of them forever. The Five Flags Inn lost its roof and an entire wall on the beach side, as the rooms filled with three feet of sand and the eerie sound of a smoke alarm pierced the desolate scene.

A truck driver plunged to his death when the cab of his truck fell from an interstate bridge that had been destroyed by Ivan. Photographs of his truck were flashed around the United States, a symbol of Ivan's fury. Divers later found the driver's body in the bay.

The damage to the Pensacola Naval Air Station was in the hundreds of millions of dollars, with many of the historic buildings badly impacted. A National Historic Landmark, the facility was a nineteenth-century shipyard before it became the country's first naval air station and pilot training center and the first naval installation to send pilots into combat. Training new naval aviators would necessarily be at a standstill for some time.

At one point Ivan was one of the most powerful hurricanes on record, weakening to some degree by the time it came ashore but still so potent that, as the eye came near to Tampa, the storm surge into Tampa Bay temporarily reversed the flow of the Hillsborough River, causing some flooding. Adding to the misery, Ivan spawned twenty-six

One of many Escambia Bay homes damaged by the storm surge
during Hurricane Ivan.
ABP PHOTO BY LINDSAY BERGSTROM, ASSOCIATED BAPTIST PRESS

tornadoes, some of them killers. In all twenty-nine people lost their
lives in Florida due to Ivan, but more deaths occurred in other parts
of the southeast and in the Caribbean.

Two hurricanes making landfall in essentially the same location in
the space of a month has never been recorded. But as Ivan became a
tropical depression and went on his way, forecasters began predicting
a category 3 storm to make landfall at Hutchison Island late Saturday
night, September 25. Hurricane Jeanne, already inflicting widespread
devastation in Haiti, was predicted to follow a path nearly identical
to Frances's. Bone-tired Treasure Coast residents, after first disbe-
lieving weather forecasters, resigned themselves and prepared again.
Evacuations this time were complicated by the fact that very few hotel
rooms were available because they were already filled with relief workers who came from out of the area to assist with previous hurricanes.

The Hurricane Center noted that from sundown Friday until sundown Saturday, September 25, was Yom Kippur, the solemn Jewish holiday when observant Jews do not listen to the radio or watch television. The center urged non-Jews to alert their Jewish friends concerning the latest situation.

Many Floridians were still without power from the last hurricane, and it certainly didn't seem fair but on Saturday, Jeanne slammed onshore near Stuart on the Treasure Coast with 120 mile per hour winds, washing out bridges, raising lake and canal levels to overflowing and causing flooding, flattening mobile homes, smashing boats, and flipping over private airplanes, cars, and trucks.

Martin, St. Lucie, and Indian River counties were in the bull's-eye, where it wasn't always possible to tell what damage had been done by Frances two weeks earlier and what was done by Jeanne. The blue plastic tarps installed on damaged roofs after Frances were in shreds, draped crazily over trees, stop signs, and pool enclosures. A Martin County official likened it to a bad dream. "We just came through people suffering ten days to two weeks of cold showers and no power. Now it's looking like that again."

When the *Miami Herald* conducted a helicopter survey, they found almost every beachfront house from Melbourne to Vero Beach had structural damage. The Florida Manufactured Housing Association estimated that one out of every five homes in the state had suffered some kind of damage in the short season. Some of the high-rise condominiums on Hutchison Island had nearly every one of their windows blown out. The storm surge forced ocean water all the way through some first floor apartments to the parking lots in back, which they buried in five or more feet of wet sand. Whole swimming pools, filled to the brim with sand instead of water, became big sand boxes at the same time as roads turned into rivers.

One unexpected misery that accompanied the disastrous summer throughout the state was the delay in conducting funerals.

Ceremonies were necessarily postponed for weeks because the ground was too wet for burials or because the families residing out of the area could not get into Florida. Frequently, undertakers were unable to find physicians to sign death certificates and were sometimes without power to refrigerate bodies or water to mix embalming fluids.

Even some artificial reefs offshore were seriously damaged by the storms because they were not in water deep enough to escape the wrath of the angry waves.

The A1A was a dangerous obstacle course with debris and dangling or downed traffic lights. In places it was hard to tell what was A1A and what was the Banana River, with calamitous results for the wrong guess. So many traffic lights were not working that virtually every intersection became a four-way stop, but police directed traffic at some of the more dangerous ones. National Guard troops in camouflage uniforms seemed to be everywhere at once, good-naturedly helping in so many ways; they were a comfort to many exhausted Floridians just by being there.

At the Vero Beach building that housed four local radio stations, the transmitting tower crashed onto the small building, nearly destroying the facility. But as the rain poured in, one of the stations, with the aid of a generator, managed to maintain contact with frightened listeners on their battery-powered radios, supplying vital information about where to get help for particular problems, what to do, and what not to do in various sticky situations.

Amazingly, Jeanne did closely follow Frances's path, but she moved almost twice as fast, much to the relief of exhausted residents. Although she left nearly 2,000 dead in Haiti, Florida's death toll was sixteen.

Then once more, the residents who played host to a hurricane, endured seemingly endless days and nights of no electricity, no safe drinking water, no ice, no air conditioning, no telephones after their cell phones ran down, no grocery stores or restaurants open, shockingly cold showers, and waiting in long lines in the blazing sun for ice, bottled water, and almost anything else they needed, because if they needed it, chances were a lot of other people needed it, too. One refrain was heard frequently from people who had elected to stay in their homes. "If there's ever another hurricane, I will run. I will never stay through another one again."

The 2004 hurricane season ended as all hurricane seasons do, in November, this one by far, the worst in modern history. Experts estimated that the hurricanes caused between $42 billion and $44 billion in damage to the state. To say something good came out of it would be difficult for the millions of people affected by it, many who, a year later, were still without functioning bathrooms or roofs that did not leak. But the public in general was much wiser in November that it had been in August. Building codes that were strengthened after Andrew in 1992 had obviously been effective and would be studied again and reinforced again if it were deemed necessary. It will be considered for some time to come as to whether manufactured homes should be permitted at all in the state.

For a brief time tourism slowed down somewhat, but as Floridians continued to rebuild and repair and the snow started falling again in the North, travelers started their annual return to the Land of Sunshine.

CHAPTER 27

"IN ORDER TO REDUCE COSTS"

The Deepwater Horizon Disaster

2010

It was early morning on April 10, 2010. The 560-million-dollar off-shore drilling rig Deepwater Horizon was stationed 4,993 feet over an oil well that extended 18,000 feet farther into the rock at the bottom of the Gulf of Mexico. A Halliburton engineer e-mailed company headquarters that the cement core installation his team had just completed had gone well.

The scene of the drilling was at a location the government called MC 252, short for "Mississippi Canyon Block 252." The name was shortened again to a code name, Macondo, in order to maintain confidentiality during early exploration.

At 9:49 p.m., a surge of methane gas erupted through the concrete, traveling up the rig to Deepwater Horizon's platform. The gas exploded into a sea of smoke and flame, killing eleven workers and injuring seventeen. The largest marine oil spill in U.S. history had begun.

Deepwater Horizon, owned by the Transocean oil-drilling company, was leased by BP, the oil company originally known as British Petroleum. Deepwater's frame soared more than twenty stories above the top of four decks—large white columns rising from immense pontoons. Weighing 33,000 tons, it was indisputability the best of Transocean's platforms. It had a crew of 130. Located on the two bottom decks were offices and living quarters; these decks contained cabins, a cafeteria, a gym, and a conference room. Service ships visited regularly with supplies, and helicopters landed on the helipad on the top deck to transport other supplies and personnel.

BP's personnel first tried to block the oil escaping from the damaged rig by using the blowout preventer. This failed, as did the attempt to install a containment dome over the biggest leak. Pumping in drilling mud and attempting to cap the blowout preventer helped some but did not solve the problem. Containment efforts continued all summer. Finally, in early September, pumping cement through a channel that connected to the damaged one permanently sealed the leak. On September 19, after two days of tests, it was announced that the Macondo 252 well was dead.

Aiming to put the best possible light on the situation, BP's earliest estimate of the amount of oil lost in the spill was ridiculously low—about one thousand barrels a day. The U.S. government had a different estimate—closer to sixty thousand barrels, or some 2.5 million gallons a day.

In May, Louisiana beaches closest to the blowout were the first to be contaminated—and the most difficult to clean because of the coast's extensive marshes, bayous, and estuaries. Tar balls and oil slicks reached the beaches of Alabama, Mississippi, and Florida in early June, polluting about 1,100 miles of shoreline.

It was a disaster. There could be no argument about that, and not much about the fact that corners had been cut and warning signs ignored when it came to safety. Originally, BP had begun drilling in October 2009 with the rig Marianas, but within a month that rig was damaged by a hurricane and had to be replaced. Deepwater Horizon took over, and on April 20 MC 252 was nearly six weeks behind schedule and fifty-eight-million dollars over budget. Investigations of BP,

Transocean, and Halliburton all disclosed facts none of them were eager to have known.

Transocean, having leased Deepwater Horizon to BP, had a well-known history of getting by with less than top-notch equipment. Shortly after the blowout it received a slightly better than "junk bond status" rating from Moody's Investors Service. As facts about the blowout became known, Transocean was shown to have ignored evidence of serious problems.

Halliburton supplied the cement used at the site of the disaster and knowingly ignored the results of tests conducted in its own lab that indicated the cement could fail, and already had done so in a similar incident in Australia.

As early as 2005, there were dramatic indications that BP was not resolutely committed to the safety of the environment or its workers. That year fifteen workers were killed and nearly 200 injured in an explosion at BP's Texas refinery. In 2006 a deteriorated pipeline in Alaska burst, spreading two hundred thousand gallons of crude oil across the snowy landscape. Also in Texas, a month before the MC 252 disaster, BP burned five hundred thousand pounds of chemicals containing cancer-causing benzene, which was released into the air and inhaled by unsuspecting residents.

Before the Deepwater Horizon disaster, the Occupational Safety and Health Administration (OSHA) released records stating that between 2007 and 2010, BP received almost half of all the safety citations issued to the entire refining business. Even more striking, BP received 760 of the total of 761 citations for the worst violations of health and safety laws. And a letter from the House Committee on Energy and Commerce to BP stated that "BP repeatedly chose risky procedures in order to reduce costs and save time and made minimal efforts to contain the added risk."

The U.S. Coast Guard responds any time a spill occurs in coastal water and did so after the Deepwater Horizon explosion and spill, rescuing survivors and, along with a Deepwater Horizon supply ship, searched for lifeboats, rafts, and missing crewmembers. As the gigantic rig leaned further and further to the side, the Coast Guard continued with dramatic search-and-rescue maneuvers while attempting to douse the fireball and skyscraper-high flames. Overhead, planes reported an oily shimmer in the water 2 miles long and half a mile wide. It took another day for the enormous rig to finally sink, gushing diesel fuel into the Gulf.

Hoping to disperse the oil before it reached land, BP sprayed enormous amounts of the chemical Corexit, even underwater, where the oil blasted from the rig. Unfortunately, as the chemical broke up and scattered the oil, the resulting small droplets worked into gullies that were home to valuable fish. The dispersants wiped out an estimated 21 percent of the oil on the water's surface, but it spread what was left over a much larger area.

There could hardly be a worse time for an offshore oil spill than springtime in the Gulf of Mexico, home to more than fifteen thousand species of wildlife. The area of MC 252 was known to have the fifth most varied assortment of marine life in the world. The Gulf also is in the direct path of millions of migrating birds on their way north. Additionally, spring is the time when many birds breed and hatch, including brown pelicans, herons, cormorants, terns, egrets, and countless others. More than eight thousand oiled birds were gathered and cleaned by volunteers, but thousands more would never be counted as they consumed oiled food, hid, died, sank, and decomposed.

In six years after the spill, the corpses of more than 1,500 dolphins and whales were found in the Gulf, the most ever counted. The National Oceanic and Atmospheric Administration (NOAA) stated that the dead creatures suffered from bacterial pneumonia or damaged adrenal glands, common results of exposure to oil. Also, almost all of the twenty-one species of dolphin and whales in the northern Gulf showed sign of injuries. The total count of dolphin deaths is assumed to be much higher, since 1,500 is only the number of dead animals that washed ashore.

At least 167,000 sea turtles died, and between two and five million larval fish were killed. Uncounted numbers of tuna, shrimp, Gulf sturgeon, crabs, red snapper, and as many as 8.3 billion oysters were lost. Injuries such as rotting fins, ugly lesions, and ingested oil have been commonly documented on fish caught by anglers.

Using remotely operated vehicles and video cameras, researchers from NOAA and Florida State University were able to discern the extensive damage done to the coral reefs and the reefs' large variety of tiny inhabitants by the oil and dispersants. Florida's coral reefs are the only barrier reefs in North America. All coral reefs grow very slowly and live for hundreds, even thousands, of years, and their deaths occur rarely. After the spill, studies found damage to coral estimated to be six hundred years old and located 67 miles from the Macondo well. It showed branches coated with mucus and a brown substance (later determined to be petroleum) and patches of discolored or dead limbs. The diversity of miniature invertebrates in or near the coral also was depleted drastically.

Although the effect of the oil and dispersants is difficult to determine in small species, it quickly became obvious that the thousands of people hired to assist in cleaning up the spill experienced rates of coughing, wheezing, and other respiratory difficulties as much as 30 percent higher than normal.

The state hardest hit by the oil spill was Louisiana, but Mississippi, Alabama, and Florida were found to have significant oil pollution; Texas suffered damage too. Conservationists believe approximately 30 percent of the oil is still unaccounted for and has possibly sunk to the ocean floor, where it can continue to do untold damage (an idea strongly opposed by the oil industry). Oil and the chemical dispersants used following the spill have been discovered in the eggs of white pelicans nesting in Illinois, Minnesota, and Iowa.

As images of tar balls washed up on beaches and birds and turtles blackened with oil spread, the fear of contamination lingered; Florida's tourism and seafood industries struggled. Restaurants closed; hotels remained empty. New damage is still being discovered—in 2014 a 1,250-pound tar mat reached Pensacola Beach and as far south as Sanibel Island.

BP, Transocean, and Halliburton continued to blame one another for the disaster until October 2015, when the largest pollution settlement in U.S. history was finalized. Transocean agreed to a one-billion-dollar civil penalty, plus a four-hundred-million-dollar criminal penalty for violating the Clean Water Act. Halliburton agreed to pay 1.1 billion dollars, plus a two-hundred-million-dollar criminal penalty for destroying evidence. BP was fined 20.8 billion dollars in damages for water pollution claims with Louisiana, Mississippi, Alabama, Florida, and Texas, as well as some four hundred local government entities.

As part of the agreement, BP must pay Florida a total of 3.2 billion dollars, an amount Florida senator Bill Nelsen stated should be much larger, for "the worst environmental disaster in history."

Bibliography

THEY NEVER SURRENDERED
No Peace Treaty with the Seminoles

Meltzer, Milton. *Hunted Like a Wolf: The Story of the Seminole War.* Sarasota,
  FL.: Pineapple Press, 2004.
Seminole Tribe of Florida, the Official Home of the Seminole Indians.
  www.semtribe.com.

DISASTER ON THE TREASURE COAST
The Wrecks of the Plate Fleet (1715)

Burgess, Robert F., and Carl J. Clausen. *Gold, Galleons & Archaeology.* New
  York: Bobbs-Merrill, 1976.
Fisher, Mel. "Mel Fisher's Historic Shipwreck Research Database."
  www.historicshipwrecks.com.
Florida Times-Union. January 29, 2001.
Gaither, Catherine M. *The 1715 Spanish Plate Fleet: Picking Up the Pieces of a
  281-Year-Old Disaster.* TuSpain.com, 1996. www.tuspain.com/heritage/
  gold.htm.
McLarty Treasure Museum. Exhibits and lecture. Vero Beach, Fla.

DISEASE SPREADS LIKE FIRE
The Yellow Fever Epidemic (1888)

Davis, T. Frederick. *History of Jacksonville, Florida and Vicinity, 1513 to 1924.*
  Third ed. Jacksonville, Fla.: San Marco Bookstore, 1990.
Fairlie, Margaret C. "The Yellow Fever Epidemic of 1888 in Jacksonville."
  Florida Historical Quarterly, Volume XIX, No. 2 (October, 1940).
Shephard, Rose. "Life History: William F. Hawley." American Life Histories:
  Manuscripts from the Federal Writers' Project, June 24, 1940.
Ward, James Robertson. *Old Hickory's Town.* Jacksonville, Fla.: Old Hickory's
  Town, Inc., 1985.

A GROWER'S NIGHTMARE
The Great Citrus Freeze (1895)

Attaway, John A. *A History of Florida Citrus Freezes.* Lake Alfred, Fla.: Science
Source, 1997.

Cook, Thomas E. *Orlando History Bit: The Big Freeze.* Orlando, Fla.: Central
Florida Heritage Foundation, 2005.

Hall, Maggi Smith, and Michael Justin Holder. *Images of America: DeLand.*
Mt. Pleasant, S.C.: Arcadia Publishing, 2003.

Mormino, Gary R. "A Ruinous Chill." *Tampa Tribune,* February 6, 2005.

Wiggins, Larry. "The Birth of the City of Miami." *Tequesta* LV (1995): 5–38.

CRANE'S OPEN BOAT
The Wreck of the Filibustering *Commodore* (1897)

Benfey, Christopher. *The Double Life of Stephen Crane.* New York: Alfred A.
Knopf, 1992.

Davis, Linda H. *Badge of Courage.* New York: Houghton Mifflin, 1998.

Katz, Joseph, ed. *The Portable Stephen Crane.* New York: Viking Press, 1969.

McCarthy, Kevin M. *Thirty Florida Shipwrecks.* Sarasota, Fla.: Pineapple
Press, 1992.

Taylor, Thomas. *Stephen Crane and the Commodore.* Ponce Inlet, Fla.: Ponce
De Leon Inlet Lighthouse Preservation Association, 1996.

Ward, James Robertson. *Old Hickory's Town.* Jacksonville, Fla.: Old Hickory's
Town, 1985.

A CITY IN FLAMES
The Jacksonville Fire (1901)

Crooks, James B. *Jacksonville after the Fire.* Gainesville: University Presses of
Florida, 1991.

Davis, Frederick T. *History of Jacksonville, Florida & Vicinity 1513 to 1924.* St.
Augustine, Fla.: The Record Company, 1925.

Foley, Bill, and Wayne Wood. *The Great Fire of 1901.* First ed. Jacksonville,
Fla.: Jacksonville Historical Society, 2001.

Ward, James Robertson. *Old Hickory's Town.* Jacksonville, Fla.: Old Hickory's
Town, 1985.

"LYNCH LAW WILL PREVAIL"
The Destruction of Rosewood (1923)

D'Orso, Michael. *Like Judgment Day.* New York: G. P. Putman's Sons, 1996.

Dunn, Marvin. *The Beast in Florida.* Gainesville, FL: University Press of Florida, 2013.

Dye, R. Thomas. "Rosewood, Florida: The Destruction of an African American Community." *The Historian,* Vol. 58, Issue 3, Tampa, FL: University of South Florida, March 1996.

Newton, Michael. *The Invisible Empire.* Gainesville, FL: University Press of Florida, 2001.

A FLOATING HOTEL SINKS
The Capsize of the *Prinz Valdemar* (1926)

Antiques Digest. "Florida—Palm Beach and the Southeast Coast, Part 1." Originally published in mid-1930s. www.oldandsold.com.

McCarthy, Kevin M. *Thirty Florida Shipwrecks.* Sarasota, Fla.: Pineapple Press, 1992.

Miami Herald. January 11–14, 1926.

Muir, Helen. *Miami, USA.* Gainesville: University Presses of Florida, 1953.

THERE WERE BODIES EVERYWHERE
The Okeechobee Dike Collapse (1928)

Barnes, Jay. *Florida's Hurricane History.* Chapel Hill: University of North Carolina Press, 1998.

Mykle, Robert. *Killer 'Cane.* New York: Cooper Square Press, 2002.

Will, Lawrence. *Okeechobee and the Hoover Dike Hurricane.* St. Petersburg, Fla.: Great Outdoors Publishing, 1961.

A BLACK WALL OF WATER
Veterans' Rescue Train Wiped Out (1935)

Barnes, Jay. *Florida's Hurricane History.* Chapel Hill: University of North Carolina Press, 1998.

"The Bonus Army." EyeWitness to History. www.eyewitnesstohistory.com (2000).

Bramson, Seth H. *Speedway to Sunshine.* Erin, Ontario, Canada: Boston Mills Press, 1944.

Eyster, Irving R. *Memorial Celebrates 60th Anniversary,* Upper Keys Independent Newspaper, Key Largo, Fla., 2005.

Gallagher, Dan. *Florida's Great Ocean Railway.* Sarasota, Fla.: Pineapple Press, 2003.

Kingseed, Wyatt. "The 'Bonus Army' War in Washington." *American History Magazine* (June 2004): 28–35.

Standiford, Les. *Last Train to Paradise.* New York: Crown Publishers, 2002.

Weaver, John B. "Hemingway and the Magazines." An Exhibition from the Speiser and Easterling-Hallman Foundation Collection of Ernest Hemingway, Columbia, S.C., University of South Carolina, 2004.

A SURPRISE ATTACK
Gulfamerica's Maiden Voyage (1942)

Dickson, Terry. "Divers Plunder Graveyard Vessels." Morris News Service. July 24, 2002. www.aiipowmis.com/inter22/in072402plunder.html.

The Fresno Bee. June 20, 2000.

Gannon, Michael. *Operation Drumbeat.* New York: Harper Collins, 1990.

Gulfstream Chapter American Merchant Marine Veterans. www.usmm.org.

New York Times. June 10, 1944.

Palm Beach Post. April 5, 2000.

St. Petersburg Times. February 10, 2003.

A GREAT AVIATION MYSTERY
The Disappearance of Flight 19 (1945)

Berlitz, Charles. *The Bermuda Triangle.* New York: Avon Books, 1975.

Bermuda Triangle Fact Sheet. Washington, D.C.: Washington Navy Yard, Naval Historical Center, 2001.

Corliss, William R. "Gas Hydrates and the Bermuda Triangle." *Science Frontiers,* No. 25 (January–Febuary 1983).

Kusche, Lawrence. *The Bermuda Triangle Mystery–Solved.* New York: Harper & Row, 1975.

————. *The Disappearance of Flight 19*. New York: Harper & Row, 1980.

Maloney, Elbert. *Chapman, Piloting, Seamanship and Small Boat Handling*. New York: Hearst, 1989.

Naval Air Station, Fort Lauderdale, Fla. Memorial Services Announcement, March 31, 2005.

A MISSION GONE WRONG
Fire in *Apollo* (1967)

Benson, Charles D., and William B. Faherty. *Moon Launch*. Gainesville: University Presses of Florida, 2001.

Cadin, Martin. *Spaceport, USA*. New York: E.P. Dutton & Co., Inc., 1959.

Drye, Willie. "The Coming of the Space Age to Cape Canaveral." *Florida Living Magazine*. August 1998: 34–39.

Jerrell, H. Shofner. *History of Brevard County*. Melbourne, Fla.: Brevard Historical Commission, 1996.

Kraft, Chris. *Flight: My Life in Mission Control*. New York: Penguin Group, 2001.

Kranz, Gene. *Failure Is Not An Option*. New York: Simon & Schuster, 2000.

Logsdon, John M. "The Space Program at 40." *Forum*, Vol. 20, No. 2 (Winter 1997–1998): 29–33.

Murray, Charles, and Catherine Bly Cox. *Apollo: The Race to the Moon*. New York: Simon & Schuster, 1989.

THE DE FACTO CAPITAL OF LATIN AMERICA
Mariel to Miami (1980)

Didion, Joan. *Miami*. New York, Simon & Schuster, 1987.

Levine, Robert M., and Moises Asis. *Cuban Miami*. New Brunswick, NJ: Rutgers University Press, 2000.

Ojito, Mirta. *Finding Manana*. New York: Penguin Press, 2005.

Rieff, David. *The Exile*. New York: Simon & Schuster, 1993.

Shell-Weiss, Melanie. *Coming to Miami*. Gainesville, FL: University Press of Florida, 2009.

THIS IS NOT A DRILL
The *Blackthorn* Collision (1980)

McCarthy, Kevin, M. *Thirty Florida Shipwrecks.* Sarasota, Fla.: Pineapple
   Press, 1992.
St. Petersburg Times. January 27, 1990, January 28, 2000, May 4, 2003, January
   27, 2005, January 29, 2005.
U.S. Coast Guard News. June 2000, September 8, 2000.

COMMUTE TURNS DEADLY
Sunshine Skyway Bridge Disaster (1980)

Cool, Kim. *Ghost Stories of Venice.* Venice, Fla.: Historic Venice Press, 2000.
Mair, George. *Bridge Down.* Briarcliff Manor, N.Y.: Stein & Day, 1982.
Marina, William F. *A History of Florida.* Third ed. Coral Gables, Fla.:
   University of Miami Press, 1999.
Save Our Seabirds. St. Petersburg, Fla.: Save Our Seabirds, Inc., 2005.
St. Petersburg Times. May 7, 2000, May 9, 1980, December 24, 1980,
   September 3, 2002.
Tampa Bay Online. January 22, 2005, April 15, 2005.

NEWS FROM LIBERTY CITY
The McDuffie Riot (1980)

Allman, T. D. *Miami: City of the Future.* Gainesville, FL: University Press of
   Florida, 1987.
Dunn, Marvin. *Black Miami in the 20th Century.* Gainesville, FL: University
   Press of Florida, 1997.
Shell-Weiss, Melanie. *Coming to Miami.* Gainesville, FL: University Press of
   Florida, 2009.
Porter, Bruce, and Marvin Dunn. *The Miami Riot of 1980.* Lexington, MA:
   Lexington Books, 1984.

A TRAGEDY FOR THE CONSTRUCTION TRADE
Harbour Cay Condominiums Collapse (1981)

Carper, Ken. "Beware of Vulnerabilities during Construction." *Seattle Daily
   Journal,* 2004.

Cocoa Beach Sentinel Star. April 4, 1981, March 21, 1982.

Today. March 28–30, 1981, April 2, 1981, April 5–6, 1981, May 1, 1981.

The Tribune. April 1, 1981.

Why Buildings Fail. Washington, D.C.: National Council of Architectural Registration Boards, 2001.

FIRE IN THE SKY
The *Challenger* Explodes (1986)

Holer, Robert T. *I Touch the Future.* New York: Random House, 1986.

Jennings, M. M. *Case Studies in Business Ethics.* Second ed. St. Paul, Minn.: West Publishing, 1996.

Kennedy Space Center. Launch information. January 28, 1986.

Kraft, Chris. *Flight: My Life in Mission Control.* New York: Penguin Group, 2001.

Kranz, Gene. *Failure Is Not An Option.* New York: Simon & Schuster, 2000.

Lewis, Richard, S. *Challenger: The Final Voyage.* New York: Columbia University Press, 1988.

Lyndon B. Johnson Space Center. Biographical data. December, 2003.

NASA. The Crew of the Challenger Shuttle Mission in 1986. NASA offices, October 22, 2004.

Orlando Sentinel. January 28, 2001.

Tallahassee Democrat. January 27, 2001.

Today. January 28–31, 1986.

Trento, Joseph J. *Prescription for Disaster.* New York: Crown Publishers, 1987.

Vaughn, Diane. *The Challenger Launch Decision.* Chicago: University of Chicago Press, 1996.

MORE THAN A STORM
Hurricane Andrew Arrives (1992)

Kleinberg, Howard. *The Florida Hurricane & Disaster 1992.* Miami, Fla.: Centennial Press, 1992.

Provenzo, Eugene F., and Asterie Baker Provenzo. *In the Eye of Hurricane Andrew.* Gainesville: University Presses of Florida, 2002.

South Florida. October, 1992.

Staff of the *Miami Herald. The Big One: Hurricane Andrew.* Miami, Fla.:
    Miami Publishing Company, 1992.
Staff of the *Sun-Sentinel. Andrew! Savagery from the Sea.* Orlando, Fla.:
    Tribune Publishing, 1992.
Sun-Sentinel. August 6, 1992, August 24–25, 1992.
USA Today. June 6, 1999.
Zarella, John. CNN.com.

A HAPPY ENDING
The Great Seabird Rescue (1993)

Exxon Valdez Oil Spill Trustee Council. *Oil Spill Facts, Questions and Answers.*
    Pamphlet published April 29, 2005 by Alaska Resources Library.
Save Our Seabirds Web site: www.seabirdrehab.org.
St. Petersburg Times. August 11–16, 1993, August 18, 1993, August 20, 1993,
    August 25–26, 1993, September 1, 1993, October 17, 1993, October 25,
    1993, January 24, 1997, October 3, 2003.

THE END OF AN AIRLINE
ValuJet Flight 592 Crashes in the Everglades (1996)

Atlantic Monthly. March 1998.
CNN Interactive News. May 11–14, 1996, May 21, 1996, May 23, 1996, May
    27, 1996, May 30, 1996, June 3–5, 1996, June 10, 1996, June 20, 1996, July
    31, 1996, September 26, 1996, November 17–19, 1996, November 22,
    1996.
Fischer, Russell. "Emergency in the Everglades." *FBI Publications* (September, 1997).
Goin, Randy, Jr. "Building to Remember," *Crit* 44 (Fall, 1999).
Miami Herald. May 15, 1996.

RED TIDE STRIKES AGAIN
Manatee Population Decimated (1996)

Environmental News Network. "Researchers Work on Red Tide Sensor."
    February 8, 2005.
Harbor Branch Oceanographic Institution. www.hboi.edu.

Kaczor, Bill. "Dolphin Deaths Likely Due to Red Tide." Associated Press, June 17, 2004.

Naples Daily News. March 15, 2005.

New York Times. April 24, 2005.

Palm Beach Post. January 24, 1998, April 6, 2005.

Sarasota Herald-Tribune. December 11, 1997, February 5, 2005, February 14, 2005.

Sierra Club. "Environmental Update." May 27, 2004.

St. Petersburg Times. March 29, 1996, April 9, 1996, April 17, 1996, May 14, 1996, July 3, 1996, September 8, 1996, December 28, 1996, January 4, 1997, January 6–7, 1997.

Tampa Tribune. August 11, 1997, January 6, 1998.

Turner, Robert. "Die-off Decimates Florida Manatee." *Endangered Species Bulletin,* XXI, no. 3.

PREDICTABLY UNPREDICTABLE WEATHER STRIKES
Killer Tornadoes (1998)

Associated Press. February 22, 1999.

CNN. "Weather Story Page." February 23–25, 1998, February 28, 1998.

Daytona Beach News-Journal. February 25, 1998, March 2–3, 1998.

Decker, Dennis. *Tornadoes.* Miami-South Florida: National Weather Service Forecast Office, 2005.

Hoover, Mark. "Tracking El Niño." *NOVA Online.* www.pbs.org/wgbh/nova/elnino/anatomy/origins.

Orlando Sentinel. February 24–25, 1998, March 1, 1998, May 31, 1998, December 27, 1998, December 30, 1998.

St. Petersburg Times. February 28, 1998.

Tampa Tribune. February 23–28, 1998, March 6, 1998.

USA Today. March 14, 2000.

FLORIDA ABLAZE
Summer of Wildfires (1998)

CNN weather story page. May 26–27, 1998, June 6–7, 1998, June 17–19, 1998, June 23, 1998, June 28, 1998, June 30, 1998, July 1, 1998, July 3, 1998. www.cnn.com/weather.

Daytona Beach News-Journal. June 21–27, 1998, June 29, 1998, July 2, 1998, July
    4–5, 1998, July 7, 1998, July 10, 1998, July 12, 1998, July 17, 1998.
EmergencyNet NEWS Services Report. June 17, 1998, Vol. 2–168.
News Hour with Jim Lehrer. Online focus. July 2, 1998.
Orlando Sentinel. April 25, 1998.
Tallahassee Democrat. April 28, 1998.

AN UNFORGETTABLE HURRICANE SEASON
Hurricanes Charley, Frances, Ivan, and Jeanne (2004)

Advisory Council on Historic Preservation. Winter 2005.
Associated Press. September 30, 2004.
CBS News. August 13, 2004, August 23, 2004.
CNN.com. August 13, 2004, August 15, 2004, September 7, 2004,
    September 13, 2004, September 24–26, 2004.
Cyber Diver News Network. August 14, 2004, October 18, 2004.
Florida Today. September 26, 2004.
Ledger. November 27, 2004.
Manufactured Housing Association. August–September 2004.
"Memorable Radio Experiences." Hurricane Season 2004, Vero Beach, Fla.,
    Treasure and Space Coast Radio Stations WGYL, WOSN, WGNX,
    and WTTB.
Miami Herald. August 16, 2004, September 3–4, 2004, September 6, 2004,
    September 10, 2004, September 17, 2004, September 19, 2004,
    September 27, 2004.
Navy Newstand. September 17, 2004, September 21, 2004.
National Geographic News. June 8, 2004, September 16, 2004.
Orlando Sentinel. September 3–4, 2004, October 3, 2004.
Palm Beach Post. September 17, 2004.
Pensacola News Journal. September 17, 2004, September 19–20, 2004,
    December 16, 2004, December 29, 2004.
Provenzo, Eugene F., and Asterie Baker Provenzo. *In the Eye of Hurricane
    Andrew.* Gainesville: University Presses of Florida, 2002.
Seattle Times. September 15, 2004.